BestMasters

Mit **„BestMasters“** zeichnet Springer die besten Masterarbeiten aus, die an renommierten Hochschulen in Deutschland, Österreich und der Schweiz entstanden sind. Die mit H’chstnote ausgezeichneten Arbeiten wurden durch Gutachter zur Ver’ffentlichung empfohlen und behandeln aktuelle Themen aus unterschiedlichen Fachgebieten der Naturwissenschaften, Psychologie, Sozialwissenschaften, Technik und Wirtschaftswissenschaften. Die Reihe wendet sich an Praktiker und Wissenschaftler gleicherma’en und soll insbesondere auch Nachwuchswissenschaftlern Orientierung geben.

Springer awards **“BestMasters”** to the best master’s theses which have been completed at renowned Universities in Germany, Austria, and Switzerland. The studies received highest marks and were recommended for publication by supervisors. They address current issues from various fields of research in natural sciences, psychology, social sciences, technology, and economics. The series addresses practitioners as well as scientists and, in particular, offers guidance for early stage researchers.

Berin Terzic · Nick King

A DLT Solution for Efficient Large-Scale Pension Administration

Springer Gabler

Berin Terzic
Finance—Dr. Christoph Kreiterling
Frankfurt School of Finance &
Management
Frankfurt, Germany

Nick King
Finance—Dr. Christoph Kreiterling
Frankfurt School of Finance &
Management
Frankfurt, Germany

This dissertation was conducted in 2024 as part of the Masters in Blockchain and Digital Assets program at the Frankfurt School of Finance & Management. It is presented as a monographic dissertation. All co-authors have made substantial contributions to the dissertation.

ISSN 2625-3577 ISSN 2625-3615 (electronic)
BestMasters
ISBN 978-3-658-48590-0 ISBN 978-3-658-48591-7 (eBook)
https://doi.org/10.1007/978-3-658-48591-7

This Springer Gabler imprint is published by the registered company Springer Fachmedien Wiesbaden GmbH, part of Springer Nature.
The registered company address is: Abraham-Lincoln-Str. 46, 65189 Wiesbaden, Germany

Executive Summary

We are facing a global pensions crisis due to the growing gap between retirement savings and retirement income requirements. The World Economic Forum identified three key factors driving the issues (World Economic Forum, 2019):

1) rapidly ageing populations due to demographic trends
2) increasing percentages of informal sector workers as industries are disrupted
3) a growing middle class throughout the world, with a corresponding increase in expectations for retirement income

These factors have also resulted in a shift from traditional government or employer-supported defined benefit (DB) pensions towards defined contribution (DC) schemes which require the individual to accumulate a pot of assets large enough to meet their needs once they retire.

This means that individuals need to take more responsibility for their own pension savings. A general lack of financial literacy and limited engagement with pensions savings makes it challenging for savers to understand how to achieve sufficient retirement savings. In response, governments have introduced policy changes, but these can have unintended consequences, such as pension savers accumulating a number of pension pots administered by different service providers (UK Government, 2023a).

During the time that these socioeconomic changes have been unfolding, there has been a significant lack of investment in technology to support pension systems, resulting in significant technical debt (Downes, 2024). This absence of infrastructure makes it challenging to find solutions to problems facing governments and pension holders and ensure adequate pension provision.

Given this backdrop, it is surprising that there has been limited research in the application of emerging technologies in the field of pensions. To address this gap, we have undertaken research in the form or case studies, expert interviews and a survey to better understand the stakeholders involved, how these interact and the key challenges that each is facing. We observe that there are multiple participants which play an important role in supporting pension plans. These participants are handling sensitive financial data that needs to be carefully stored and transferred between these participants. Further, each participant is operating separate closed databases which require communications to coordinate and reconcile. Inefficiencies in the foundational architecture of pensions systems results in unnecessary expense and slow transaction processing, meaning a poor experience for pension holders.

We explore the potential for cloud-based and DLT technologies to address some of these issues. We apply Socio-Technical and Structuration theories to explore the interplay of social and technical elements of pensions systems and how open systems can provide benefits. Cloud-based infrastructure can offer some improvement in data accessibility and transferability but will generally still require separate, closed instances of pension holder data that needs to be coordinated, meaning that the impact will be limited. A DLT-based solution can facilitate a shared database/ledger across the various participants in the system. This would improve efficiency in the operational model by reducing the level of manual administration and communication required between pension plans. It would also enable accurate, up-to-date and consistent information to be held about plan members. Not only would this help members to better understand the total value of their pension savings, but this transparency will also ensure that investment policy and asset allocation is appropriate at an aggregate level rather than considering each pension separately. Ensuring optimal asset allocation and risk management can result in a better level of pension assets accumulated at retirement. This reporting would also be easily accessible to other stakeholders such as regulators and tax authorities.

We recognise that pension systems are highly regulated and many of the participants are often highly risk-averse and resistant to change. We therefore propose that the solution is implemented in two steps. The first step to implement a platform for the sharing of information on a 'read-only' basis, providing some immediate efficiency gains and also allowing stakeholders to interact in a very risk-controlled way. Once all stakeholders are comfortable with the read-only shared infrastructure and this has demonstrated the expected value, they should progress to the full 'read/write' shared ledger. This approach is also likely to be preferable to regulators as they are able to monitor progress and evolve regulations over time as the solutions become proven.

Abstract

This body of work investigates potential solutions for efficient large-scale pension administration. It reviews the historical and current significance of pensions in everyday society as well as the interactions between the pensioners and the pension structure. This is done in the growing context of a 21st century pension crisis from a demographic standpoint and lack of ongoing technological implementation. Pensioners, governments, regulatory authorities, pension administrators and more stakeholders face several challenges in looking to the future of the pension system which is slowly creating societal imbalances.

In incorporating evidence from field research (in the pension and technology sectors), case studies in single country pension systems, case studies in multi-country systems, a practical end-to-end case study and expert interviews, this body of work validates that distributed ledger technology (DLT) is an efficient solution for large-scale pension administration. Additionally, through cross-comparisons of other technological solutions available such as cloud technology and analysis from Socio-Technical Theory and Structuration Theory, the implications of using DLT technology are widespread and beneficial in a societal and structural context. There are concerns evident with the implementation of this technology demonstrated through regulatory processes, it being an experimental technology and legacy infrastructure, corporations which tend to be risk-averse in the field of pensions.

Contents

Abbreviations

BPL	Blockchain Platform
BTA	Blockchain Transfer Agent
DB	Defined Benefit
DC	Defined Contribution
DLT	Distributed Ledger Technology
GUI	Graphical User Interface
IRM	International Retirement Migration
OECD	Organisation for Economic Co-operation & Development
PP	Pension Provider
STS	Socio-Technical Theory
TA	Transfer Agent
WEF	World Economic Forum
Wtp	Wet toekomst pensioenen

List of Figures

List of Tables

1 Introduction & Background

The concept of a pension plan seems to be inherently interwoven to the societal fabric that comes with full time employment. Although it seems this way in modern times, the concept of a pension is fairly new. The roots of the idea were laid in 1881 as a concept and in 1889 as a practical implementation where Germany is touted to be the first nation to adopt such a system (as designed by Otto von Bismarck). The purpose of the system was to promote well-being of the working class and encourage maximum operating efficiency of the German economy. Mandatory participation and a system of income security would prove to be the cornerstone of Bismarck's pension system; these basic fundamentals would then drive pension systems and revolutions deep into the 20th century (Mierzejewski, 2016). Through technological and ideological revolutions, pension systems found themselves profoundly impacted either through intrinsic systemic changes (such as pension reforms in the creation of additional structures or pillars such as the conceptualisation of defined contribution plans) or through technological revolutions that fast-tracked the ability of pension contributions and distributions (Verbon, 1987). Since the early days of the pension system, there have been many successes and failures of these systems both in private and public landscapes and as society nears the 150-year mark of working pension systems, it is natural that there is a revolution of how they operate. Before we engage down the path of revolution, we must assess where pensions have come today.

Pensions are designed to provide a reliable source of income during retirement, allowing individuals to maintain their standard of living when they stop working, or reduce working hours. Therefore, pensions fulfil a critical role in ensuring financial security and societal welfare (Terziev, 2019). At the same time, pensions

B. Terzic and N. King, *A DLT Solution for Efficient Large-Scale Pension Administration*, BestMasters, https://doi.org/10.1007/978-3-658-48591-7_1

systems are complex, making them difficult for individuals to understand and assess if they have the necessary provisions in place.

Through a series of case studies and expert interviews, we will explore the structure of pensions across geographies, the different stakeholders involved and how these interact. We will investigate some of the challenges faced as pension systems are evolving and potential solutions. We will first briefly explore how pensions are structured, and this will elucidate the structural tie with the engagement of the individual actors and stakeholders within the process.

1.1 How Pensions are Structured

There is significant variation in how pension systems are structured globally reflecting the socioeconomic context of each country. In general, pension systems comprise three pillars:

1. State-provided Pension
   The first pillar pension is provided by the state and is designed to provide a basic level of income to retirees. It is generally unfunded which means that there is no underlying pool of assets or investments to pay pension benefits. Instead, mandatory contributions paid by current workers and employers (for example, National Insurance contributions in the UK) are used to pay the benefits of retirees. Where the current contributions are not sufficient to pay the required benefits, these will generally be supplemented by tax revenues.
2. Employment-based/occupational based pensions
   The second pillar pension is provided as part of employment benefits and typically funded by contributions paid by employers and employees, which are then invested to accumulate a pool of assets to pay pension benefits. These can either be Defined Benefit (DB) or Defined Contribution (DC) pension plans.

   DB plans provide a defined level of income in retirement, generally based on a formula which considers salary and length of service with the employer. These provide certainty and security to employees but place significant risk on employers as they have the responsibility to accumulate the assets required to pay the benefits through their contributions and investment returns.

   Under a DC plan, the pension income will depend upon the contributions that have been paid during employment and the investment returns achieved on these. This places the responsibility on employees to ensure that they have sufficient assets to provide the required income. The employee will often be able to set their own levels of contributions and also determine how assets are invested. This provides a lot of flexibility but requires the employee to understand the responsibilities that they are taking on.

3. Individual savings and investments
   The final pillar comprises additional voluntary savings and assets that the retiree has accumulated to supplement the benefits provided by the state and employers. This could be a wide range of assets including cash savings, investments and real estate.

1.2 Socioeconomic Change and a Global Pensions Crisis

There is growing gap between retirement savings and retirement income requirements which according to The World Economic Forum (WEF) is creating a looming pensions crisis (World Economic Forum, 2019). The WEF identified three key factors driving the issues:

1. Rapidly ageing populations due to demographic trends
2. Increasing percentages of informal sector workers as industries are disrupted
3. A growing middle class throughout the world, with a corresponding increase in expectations for retirement income.

According to the WEF report, the pensions funding gap is expected to grow to $400 trillion by 2050 (World Economic Forum, 2019).

These factors also mean that governments and employers are unable to bear the cost or risks of the state pensions or DB pension plans which have historically given certainty of income to retirees and required limited financial literacy or involvement from them.

We are therefore seeing increasing importance of employer DC plans and third pillar individual savings. The Organisation for Economic Co-operation and Development (OECD) notes that DC plans "are increasingly an integral part of most countries' overall pension system, and in some countries, they are the main component of their pension system. Therefore, overall retirement income adequacy depends on the retirement income stemming from these plans" (OECD, 2024).

This means that individuals are having to take more responsibility for their own pension savings in order to accumulate a pot of assets large enough to meet their needs once they retire. This is challenging as a general lack of financial literacy and limited engagement with pensions savings makes it challenging for savers to understand how to achieve sufficient retirement savings.

Given the increasing focus on employment-based DC plans and the unique challenges that these present, we will focus our research here. There is clearly a need to make these pensions more transparent, accessible and easier to understand.

1.3 Pensions & Technology

In understanding the above challenges, we need to look to the scales of evolution and technology in pensions to identify the starting point to how we can begin to classify transparency, accessibility and ease of system comprehension. Pension systems have evolved into the three pillars that we see before us in each society's plans. What is often forgotten is the hand-in-hand technological evolution that is driving the system infrastructure ensuring that pensions can continue on an evolutionary conquest. With the advancement of pension ideologies and the start to a shift to DC structured plans in the late 20th century, the technology surrounding pension administration has needed to keep pace to ensure accurate provision of pensions.

For the most part at each pension revolution there was a symbiosis with technological revolution in the space. Notably throughout the 20th century there was the computer revolution which epitomised at the turn of the century for pensions: capturing large amounts of data onto servers for pension administration created a more effective way to manage data, transfer funds and disburse pensions. Since then, the pension industry has been seen as not stepping in pace with technological revolution and has been cited as building up "technical debt" (Downes, 2024). This elegant symbiosis has apparently stagnated in the 21st century and has become amensalism where the complexity of the pension system is increasingly eating away at any technological revolution that is attempting to drive efficiency. Large swathes of data, long lead times, an inefficient end-to-end pension process mean that we are observing a technological crisis that is compounding the pension funding crisis that we described in the previous section.

As part of closing the technological gap, we believe that there is significant scope for a solution to help increase transparency and make it easier for individuals to understand their pension savings, particularly when this may come from multiple sources. This is tied to the need for data accessibility and the concurrent loss of technological advancement in the pension space.

Available Literature in the Field 2

Pensions fulfil an essential role in creating safety for individuals' financial security and safety for overall societal stability and welfare. As such, it is only natural to find the most effective and efficient way in delivering such a system to the populace. While the discussion of pensions and increasing efficiencies through potential technology implementations are extremely important, research remains extremely niche and unfocused on specialties. Kamal et al confirm this in their 2023 paper that there is a lack of research in applying DLT or any blockchain technology in the area of pension systems (Kamal, et al., 2023). The limited research to date has been highly theoretical with limited examples of practical applications or benefits to individuals. If one takes a step to view the research space, pensions have lengthy documentation which is academically driven in understanding history and arrival to the modern pension system (Verbon, 2012); however, as the purpose of the research that is engaged in these pages the focus is different and the breadth of research available in the pension space has limited applicability in defining pension system DLT based efficiencies. As a result, this body of work will include a mix of research rooted in secondary sources that are not only academic journals or research papers.

Consequently, due to the need for a variety of sources, a mixed methods approach is employed because of inherent limitations of resource availability in the academic field of study (DLT and pensions). To effectively understand pensions at breadth, this research paper will rely on academic, peer-reviewed journals and books. In order to supplement to address the DLT topics, this paper will take the further step to pull primary source information from migration databases (United Nations Global Migration Database), conduct expert interviews, conduct a survey, pull from secondary source articles, creation of select

B. Terzic and N. King, *A DLT Solution for Efficient Large-Scale Pension Administration*, BestMasters, https://doi.org/10.1007/978-3-658-48591-7_2

case studies and limited whitepapers. The conducted interview experts will supplement "real-world" examples and be an effective data source for potential field implementations of a DLT based pension solution and how the current system is perceived and functioning. Further, the survey information will aim to create a broader basis of quantitative information that can be cross-compared with the Global Migration Database; this in turn create a source of fundamental information in understanding how migratory movements would need to be considered in a DLT based pension system as it drives understanding in the scope of efficient DLT based pension systems (whether consideration exists for cross country comparisons or only within one country market). This will allow for a holistic study of information that is currently available—as it is not directly available in the non-established, niche academic field of DLT based pension systems.

2.1 Findings from Selected Sources

This research paper works to set a basic understanding of pension system history, the modern pension system and what an efficient DLT based solution would resemble. In the former category, Verbon's, Mierzejewski's, Terziev's works are used to understand the history of the evolution of pension systems and a basis for the current systemic infrastructure. Given the complexity of such a theoretical description, the conducted expert interviews serve to provide a true, complete description of the current system.

With the establishment of a basis in understanding pension systems, Brenna (2003) and Blommestein et al (2009) supplement the conversation in defining the inherent differences of the three pension pillars and provide clarity in which pillar would benefit most in the immediate rollout of DLT based pension platforms. The result, in short, is that Defined Contribution plans would be the most suitable for innovation in efficient management; this is also the defining characteristic in the case studies written in this paper.

In assessing a true, effective solution to solve the problem of inefficient pension administration it is also necessary to look at potential solutions that are currently in use or could be in use as a piece of financial technology that seeks to target the same systemic inefficiencies. Therefore, this paper also leverages research in the area of cloud networks which may provide a form of solution that competes with DLT based provision; thus, it is important to assess the solutions of a DLT and cloud based system in direct comparison to ensure that not only is the DLT system efficient for large scale pension administration, but that there is no direct alternative to resolving the intrinsic issues in the today's system.

Notably we did find mentions of a new, experimental solution hybridising cloud architecture with a DLT solution by Stanke et al. (2020), Westerlund & Kratzke (Westerlund & Kratzke, 2018) and Trautmann's overview on the general evolution of cloud computing compared to distributed ledger technology (Trautmann, 2023); however, these conversations have remained majority theoretical and on an elementary level when compared to the body of research on theoretical and practical implementations of DLT and Cloud technology separately.

Furthermore, to identify a layer more specific to DLT based solutions in the space, we look to the limited research that is currently available. Sestoft (2017) is considered one of the earliest research projects into the DLT Pension field, they described the core activities of a pension and proposed, at a high level, how these could be implemented autonomously using DLT. This provided arguments for why the technology is suitable but very limited information of the actual implementation or practical benefits. Moreover, Schubert and Perret used the OECD's ten recommendations for the good design of DC pension plans as a framework for a series of expert interviews to explore opportunities for the application of blockchain technology for improving these plans (Schubert & Perret, 2024). Through these interviews they concluded that there are opportunities for "improvements in cost structure and efficiency, as well as in the management and monitoring of pension plans". However, they did not describe how any of these improvements could be implemented.

Sarker and Datta have provided a comprehensive proposal for a blockchain-based pension administration infrastructure (2022). They concluded that "high administrative costs and associated operational inefficiencies present multiple challenges for pension industries across different countries. Although blockchain is considered a potential solution for these concerns, the pension industry has not fully leveraged this disruptive technology." The paper is very much focused on the technical implementation rather than exploring the practical problems that we are trying to solve. At the same time, Sarker and Datta provide a great summary of the many participants involved in pension provision. However, there are a couple of important omissions. First of all, there is no mention of the member's important role in determining how their assets are invested in the case of DC plans. Secondly, the role of Transfer Agents maintaining registers of holdings. Overall, there are sources we can draw from to create assumptions and when coupled with case studies it will lead to a greater beneficial discourse in the pursuit of academic truth.

2.2 Research Conducted within this Body of Work

In identifying the clear limitations of the existing body of research and attempting to create a solid foundation for the argument of a future solution for efficient pension administration, research was conducted directly in relation to this thesis. We conducted a survey, three expert interviews, and analysed four case studies to ensure that this paper is able to aid in furthering the field of study. The aim of these individual research studies is to combine specific elements mentioned in the Socio-Technical Systems Theory (STS) and Structuration Theory that we are using as theoretical frameworks for understanding technology, tasks, people and structure interactions as this is important for the pension ecosystem.

It is important to indicate that in the survey we had n = 20 participants which constitutes a limited view of the field, however it is important nonetheless. It provides necessary information on an individual basis of the respondents, and it provides a landscape correlation assessment; one of which we found enforces the already available statistics from the Global Migration Database. We found the need to engage in this survey driven by a lack of widely available data for understanding the scope of persons that live abroad and have contributed to more than one pension system in their professional lives. Further, it gave better ties to the overall understanding of a key point in Structuration theory of Time-Space Distanciation in identifying the nature of shrinking distance between cultural systems by showcasing cross border work trends and indicating interactions across systems (e.g. globalisation impacts). Finally, we do need to acknowledge that there is a limitation due to the method of survey interviewing is anonymous self-reporting. This may introduce bias or inaccuracies in the data source, however overall we still find the nature of the case study, when paired with the others, integral to our research.

Moreover, the expert interviews aid in creating a qualitative picture of the current financial field as it related to a potential solution and further development of such in this space. Notably, three interviews were conducted. The number of interviews does not provide extensive information, yet it was difficult to find experts that would be able to discuss pensions and potential DLT solutions given the particularity of the field; as a result, three interviewees were chosen to ensure high quality remained from the expert sources and these three interviewees represented a high-calibre, senior representation of key stakeholders in pension infrastructure. These interviewees were the best fit because between them they provided three specific viewpoints: a social view, a technical view and a stakeholder approach. Since the theoretical basis of the paper hinges on the cross-interaction of stakeholders and structural systems at its core, the interviewees supplemented through the lens of a real-world view to this theoretical implementation. This is especially noticeable as the experts were direct in feedback about the engagement with potential prototypical systems in the pension space while also commenting on the current structural landscape specific to their fields. They further balanced the limitations of research in the space as they were able to directly comment on the topics as senior experts in their respective fields. We had considered other possibilities on interviewees; however, these were more theoretical in nature and with less direct field experience as those we could find directly for the purpose of this research. Having these specific expert interviewees created a holistic overview that could be extrapolated against the research we were able to identify as relevant.

Finally, the four case studies (UK Case Study, Netherlands Case Study, Cross Country Pension Contributions, Process of Transferring a Pension within a Single Market Case Study) support with a concrete analysis of both singular and multi market approaches for pension systems. What is important to mention, these four case studies were selected to provide a very specific, complete overview of the situation. The UK & Netherlands case studies were selected as both give a specific single market overview of the pension situation and both are able to be cross-compared extensively—other countries were considered, however these two were chosen given strong, systemic reforms in recent years, diversity in pension systems (strong coverage in all three pillars), the United Kingdom's request for proposals surrounding technological systems to support the pension systems and the consideration of Blockchain technology already by the market in the Netherlands study. The situation in the UK is a look into the past and present as the system had an overhaul two decades ago leading to the current system in use; while the Netherlands situation is one looking forward to potential implications of the introduction of a reformed pension system and what potential results of such a change will incur on the structure and the people engaging with the system. For the third case study, Cross Country Pension Contributions, we decided to also look at a global angle as there is a significant movement of peoples across several pension systems and what this would mean. The purpose was to understand the scale of the demographic and impact in order to assess what kind of solution would be needed. Additionally, the case study aided in looking cross-borders to structures that exist in the global sphere in line with conceptualisation from Giddens' Structuration Theory. For example, whether the issues lie in cross country pension topics or whether targeting a single country pension system is where the majority of the issues arise based on those interacting with the system (and understanding the tie with the concept of Time-Space Distanciation). Finally, to ensure that there is a clear identification of the process on a singular individual, we have run a case study on the process of transferring a pension within a single market to understand what such a process looks like and the lead times surrounding the process. This was done as we want to understand if there are limitations and lengthy lead times for individual engagements with pension systems. We directly utilised one of our case study countries for this, as it would provide a parallel between identification of the structure of the system and the individual's agency within the system. For all the aforementioned case studies, we did consider other potential scenarios to create a similar overview which we could use in combination with the other research and theoretical frameworks, however this fell short of the expectations we had for potential cross-assessment and real market scenarios. For example, we did consider other ways to convey the inefficient pension structure such as data points or information we looked to in our research, but we found running an actual end-to-end study of a person who was attempting to get their pension transferred would be much more valuable as a research point and similar to the cross-country pension comparisons of 'mock' scenarios between countries; this helped facilitate a clearer view rather than simply referencing this within the paper. It helped us garner much more practical information throughout the process such as the length of it; we wanted to ensure that we had great theoretical foundations and were able to connect this to practical scenarios. This is especially since the theoretical frameworks we chose had an explicit emphasis on stakeholder interaction with structures and in engaging in practical research we were able to infer what potential impacts arise between engagements in the system. This is the main reason we took the real examples of the UK, Netherlands as they are undergoing transformations (or have undergone them) where we can directly assess the stress put on the pension structures which need to be alleviated for the best stakeholder and system interaction. Each case study we undertook created a piece of the wider overview from single markets to multi-markets, from individuals to multiple societies bridging the theoretical with practical research.

The purpose of the research available and the research that is needed to be conducted as part of the topic is a clear indication that there is an essential gap within the pension field, the gap of research and formulations surrounding DLT based pension solutions. It is to this reason why the research of this paper is fundamental to furthering the pension space and more specifically the DLT pension industry. Research builds the necessary basis for our understanding of the landscape in pensions, in DLT and closely related areas. We identified that pensions systems play an integral role within society that we need to assess how to better. As a result, we look to stating a growing gap that we recognised and identify whether a solution that we propose (based on our research body) would efficiently service this.

3 Research Question & Hypothesis

Pension systems play an important role in ensuring financial security and societal welfare of individuals. At the same time, pensions arrangements are complex, difficult to understand and inefficient due a lack of transparency and the use of separate, closed technology platforms used by different stakeholders.

Through our research, we seek to understand the challenges faced in pensions provision, the different stakeholders involved and the existing infrastructure. We would then like to explore if a DLT solution could be implemented for pension administration to increase efficiency and improve outcome for pension holders. Our hypotheses are as follows:

H_0: DLT solutions offer no efficiency gains for pension administration compared to legacy infrastructure.

H_1: If pension administration is implemented using a DLT solution then there could be greater transparency, efficiency and an improved outcome for pension holders.

This research question is designed to explore how emerging technologies can be used to improve social outcomes. We will therefore use Socio-Technical Systems (STS) Theory as a theoretical framework for our research alongside a model that offers insight on human behaviour within a structural model (Structuration theory). STS emphasises the interrelatedness of social and technical aspects of an organisation or system making it an ideal framework for exploring our research question, which is exploring application of emerging technologies to pensions (a key component of societal welfare systems). In addition, structuration theory assesses the duality of structures between the individual's agency (or actions) in

B. Terzic and N. King, *A DLT Solution for Efficient Large-Scale Pension Administration*, BestMasters, https://doi.org/10.1007/978-3-658-48591-7_3

relation to the societal structures in place; this makes it a powerful secondary framework as it looks to identify the dichotomy between people and system—which in this case is the impact of human behaviour on the pension system and the rigor of the pension system for humans.

3.1 Socio-Technical Systems (STS) Theory

The STS theory is built on work by Harold, J. Leavitt in the 1960s. Leavitt's Diamond model states that successful change management requires consideration of four key elements: people, tasks, structure and technology. The model proposed that these elements each have an impact on the others and successful change requires a balance between them (Fig. 3.1).

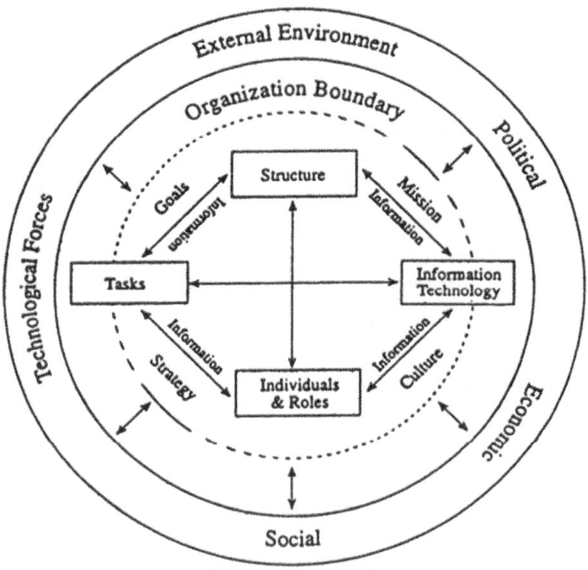

Fig. 3.1 STS Organisation Interaction Model (Wigand, 2007)

In the context of our research:

Structure represents the overall pension system including the different components, stakeholders, hierarchies and interactions.

Task refers to the activities being performed by the pension system. There are many here, but these are ultimately leading to the main task of pensions provision.

Technology refers to the systems and infrastructure that is being used to perform the task of pensions provision.

People are the different individuals involved in the pension system, the most important being pension holders.

According to Pasmore et al. the socio-technical approach is a

> "method of viewing organisations which emphasises the interrelatedness of the functioning of the social and technological subsystems of the organisation and the relation of the organisation as a whole to the environment in which it operates. Put simply, the sociotechnical system perspective contends that organisations are made up of people that produce products or services using some technology, and that each affects the operation and appropriateness of the technology as well as the actions of the people who operate it." (Pasmore et al, 1982).

Some key concepts of STS Theory are:

1. **Joint Optimisation**—The optimal performance of a system is achieved when the social and technical elements are jointly optimised.
2. **Open Systems**—Preference for systems which involve flow and interaction between components of the system or structure.

By applying STS Theory to our research, we will explore the interplay of social and technical elements of pensions systems and how open systems can provide benefits. Given the critical socioeconomic role played by pensions systems, the concept of joint optimisation is highly relevant as we need to ensure that any technological improvements also lead to direct benefits to pension plan members.

3.2 Structuration Theory

The Structuration theory was developed by Anthony Gidden and is extensively presented in his book The Constitution of Society (1984). Structuration theory looks to build a bridge between agency and structure. More importantly, sociologists were seeing the two as separate, however Gidden's proposes that these are related, are part of a wider duality and not in opposition to each other. We see this identified in the following figure (Fig. 3.2):

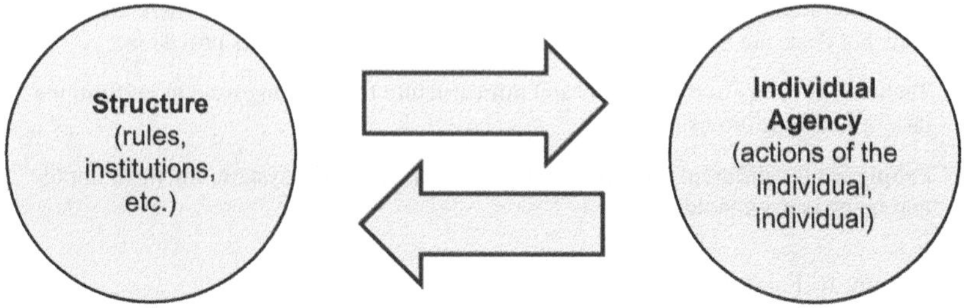

Fig. 3.2 The Duality of Structure

The duality of structure, in the theory that Gidden's proposes, is similar to having a sword where the hilt is as important as the blade; where the blade and hilt both impact the balance of the wider weapon. In a similar way, both structure and individual agency have lasting impacts on each other as is showcased above: the individual's actions can impact and/or change the structure while the structure through rules and institutions creates a stable system that exists with or without the individual. In short, actions can impact, change, mirror the structure and the structure enables such actions while also posing constraints by regulations that can make actions palatable for others.

Specifically, within our research we can identify the duality of structure and agency quite well. The structure is the rules, regulations and wider institution of a pension system. The individual agency is the person(s) engaging within the system. Importantly, we can see fundamental impacts that individual agency has had on pension systems through the demographic shifts in age across countries which puts pressure on the structure.

There are 2 vital key concepts that are presented through the Structuration theory that we need to keep central to our discussions:

1. **Time-Space Distanciation:**
   a. "the stretching of social systems across time-space, on the basis of mechanisms of social and system integration" (Gidden p. 377, 1948);
   b. This is the concept that modern societies diminish the distance between them and the time to cross-communicate. This is due to globalisation impacts as well as the development of technology.
2. **Reflexive Monitoring:**
   a. This is indicated by Gidden as the self-regulation of individuals as they progress or move through modern society. Individuals look to critically

assess their own actions within a broader social context. This is key to the agency as it creates significant response to structures, events, situations.

b. The individual actively (re)shapes social structures.

In applying the theoretical framework to our research and study, it is important to note that it is not without critiques, and we need to recognise these as it may change the limitations of our assessment. One of the main critiques is arising from Archer as they wrote

> "Structural influences thus extend beyond T^2 and it is essential to know whether this is because they (temporally and temporarily) resist collective pressures to change, remain because they represent vested interests of the powerful, or are in fact 'psychologically supported' by the population. To regard every institutional regulatory as the result of 'deep sedimentation' is to assimilate them all to the latter category. Yet without these distinctions it remains inexplicable when (or whether) the property will be transformed." (Realist Social Theory: The Morphogenetic Approach, 1995, p. 78)

In short, we need to be aware that there are foundations to structures that can be resistant to change even with immense pressure; the capacity of such structures in certain cases has fundamental resistance to change. For example, if a government system forces structure, it is unlikely that this system will be shaped or reshaped by the actions of the individuals, and it forms an imbalanced system (models of economic institutions similar to the USSRs can be used as examples or akin to slavery institutions). A more direct example within the discussion in the pages of this body of work is the relationship between pensions and demographics of a country population: when there is an aging population due to the actions of the individual it creates a reshaping of the pension structure to ensure future viability.

Through the use of Structuration theory as a secondary model, we can build on the analysis by the STS theory in looking specifically to the people component and the interrelationship of socio-economic interactions with the pension structure. This will allow us to more clearly define the role of the structure and agency, that the best solution is able to be malleable to this duality.

Evidence & Problem Statement 4

In order to assess whether there are opportunities to find potential solutions to increase efficiencies in pension systems, we have analysed relevant case studies and also conducted interviews with key stakeholders to gather their insights and perspectives.

4.1 UK Case Study

Like many other countries, pension provision in the UK is structured around the three pillars set out in the introduction. Increased life expectancy and an ageing population has put increasing pressure on the state-provided pension in the UK. This has resulted in the UK government increasing retirement age to ensure viability of the pension system. At the same time, the UK government is seeking to reduce reliance on the first pillar pension, increasing the importance of occupational and personal savings.

Recognising that the current level of occupational pension benefits is insufficient to offset the pressure on the public pension system, the Pensions Act 2008 introduced a requirement that employees that are earning over £10,000 per year and between the age of 22 and pensionable age are automatically enrolled into a pension plan provided by their employer, unless they opt out (UK Government, 2022). This change was designed to increase the participation rate of pension

Supplementary Information The online version contains supplementary material available at https://doi.org/10.1007/978-3-658-48591-7_4.

B. Terzic and N. King, *A DLT Solution for Efficient Large-Scale Pension Administration*, BestMasters, https://doi.org/10.1007/978-3-658-48591-7_4

savings and was phased in over a five-year period beginning on the 1st of January 2012, starting with the largest firms and requiring smaller firms to comply over time.

This Automatic Enrolment programme has been very successful, increasing participation rates from 55% in 2012 to 88% in 2021 (UK Government, 2021). The impact has been most pronounced for 'low earners and multiple job holders, women, ethnic minorities and other under pensioned groups who are making minimal pension contributions and who move jobs more frequently due to insecurity of part-time work' (UK Government, 2023c).

However, there has been a cost of this change as it has resulted in a large number of sub-scale pensions pots being created as employees move between employers. These pots are not cost-effective for pension administrators to support and are creating an inefficiency in the pension system. The UK Government issued a call for evidence in January 2023 and data from a number of pension administrators highlighted the size of the issue with around 20 million deferred pension pots worth less than £10,000, representing an estimated £30 billion of assets (UK Government, 2023b).

Table 4.1 Pension Pot Volume across Pot size and Asset Value

Pot Size	Number of Pots	Estimated Value of Assets
Below £1,000	12.1 million	£4.2 billion
Between £1,000 and £2,500	3.8 million	£6.1 billion
Between £2,500 and £5,000	2.3 million	£7.8 billion
Between £5,000 and £10,000	3.8 million	£6.1 billion

A further issue is that employees are losing track of their pension savings, with the PPI estimating in 2022 that the total value of lost pension pots was more than £26 billion (Pensions Policy Institute, 2022).

In an attempt to address these issues, the UK Government has initiated the Pensions Dashboard Programme which aims to allow savers to access information on all of their occupational and state pension savings in one place and locate lost pension pots.

Whilst this is a significant step forward in providing transparency into pensions savings, it does not address the inefficiencies that result from multiple small pots.

In June 2022, the Small Pots Industry Coordination Group estimated that by 2030 this will result in 'wasted administration costs third of a billion pounds per annum' (UK Government, 2023a). This will increase costs for savers and also could impact the viability of pension providers, reducing choice.

Several different models have been proposed to address the issue of small, deferred pots (UK Government, 2023a):

- **Default Consolidator**—Under this model, pots which meet certain criteria will be automatically transferred to a consolidator, unless the saver opts-out.
- **Pot Follows Member**—Under this model, when an employee moves jobs, their existing pension pot will transfer to their new employer's pension plan.
- **Member Exchange**—Under this model, pension providers would use a 'trusted third party pseudonymised data service' to identify where they have a deferred pot, and another provider has an active pot for the same pension saver.

The UK Government decided that the Default Consolidator approach is the most appropriate immediate solution (UK Government, 2023c), balancing the need to address the issue of small, deferred pots and protecting outcomes for pension savers. A further consultation explored the implementation of this approach, and a key issue identified the importance of 'having a central point or system to manage and match data' (UK Government, 2023c). Two options were proposed:

- A **central clearing house** which would match deferred pots and coordinate the consolidation, communicating with the pension saver.
- A **central registry** which pension administrators could use to identify where pots should be consolidated.

Most respondents to the consultation supported the clearing house approach, stating that it would be simpler for pension administrators as they 'would set up systems to interact with a single organisation' rather than 'multiple potential competitors' (UK Government, 2023d). However, other respondents raised concerns regarding how this approach would be funded to 'create and develop systems, with the necessary automated processes, as well as ongoing costs … of data storage, system maintenance and administrative costs'.

Interestingly, a DLT solution was not mentioned, even though this would seem to achieve the best of both proposed solutions.

4.2 Netherlands Case Study

4.2.1 The Theory

As is similar to the case in the United Kingdom with the Pension Act of 2008, the Dutch government approved plans to create a substantial systemic change with a new pension system. The new pension system arises from a need as the Dutch market faces challenges that result from an overall aging population, longer working hours, and lower employee retention rates (the employee is more likely to change firms sooner). The Future Pension Act (Wet toekomst pensioenen) came into effect on July 1, 2023 and expects full implementation by January 1, 2028 when unions, employers and the pension providers are expected to fully comply and adapt their pension plans from defined benefit pensions (pension entitlements) to a defined contribution plan (personal pension pots) (Rijksoverheid Nederland, 2023).

The Wet toekomst pensioenen (Wtp) regulation has an impact of roughly 70% of Dutch employees which currently participate in a DB plan; therefore, within the Wtp it sets forth 3 transitional periods to ensure that the adjustment to DC plans is done effectively:

1. **1st of January 2025:** "Employment Benefit Phase" in which individual employer, social partners create agreements on new pensions plans and designing the transition plan.
2. **1st of July 2025:** "Accommodation Phase" in which pension providers prepare an implementation plan (based on step 1).
3. **1st of January 2028:** "Implementation Phase" in which pensions are now in a DC plan with "age-independent flat contributions".

While the transition changes the baseline for pension plan schemes, it is also changing regulation surrounding the plans themselves. Wtp amends the concept of a contribution rate (the uniform premium) and instead rolls in a flat-rate contribution that is independent of age—with a maximum premium of 30% of pensionable salary. It also changes the minimum entry age from 21 to 18 years as of January 1st, 2024 (citigroup, 2023).

While, as illustrated above, the Wtp changes several other regulations, the biggest impact is not merely the move from DB to DC but the fundamental adjustment from one large pension fund to several individual pension funds. In other words, there is a move from centralisation of pension funds per each pension provider to having individual pension pots for every participant. Functionally this allows for more personalised information about employees and their pension accruals, however logistically it can be extremely challenging to implement. In addition, there needs to be a full overview of the individual pension participant that is readily accessible and up to date with validated information; this means a full transparent and complete overview of the individual's pension participation.

To put the impact of the pension plan transition into perspective it will have very real impacts for all stakeholders involved in the pension plan process:

- **Individual**:
  a. Will need to understand every single DC plan they are/have been a part of in their working career. This results in a lengthy tracking of history and any DC plans that they have contributed to at any point in their working career.
  b. Need access to up-to-date information.
- **Corporates**:
  a. Implementation of new infrastructure and relationship with pension plan providers. The competition for new employees will take place on the field of pension provision as plans are more portable which means more transparency is needed.
  b. Reduced liability as investment risk is borne by the policyholders themselves.
  c. Increased cost predictability for the corporate entities as they commit to a defined contribution amount to the employees' pension pots instead of guaranteeing specific retirement benefits.
- **Pension Plan Providers:**
  a. Creation of individual pension pots that every single individual participant is able to manage their own accrued assets (systemic overhaul).
  b. Accessibility of assets is more fundamental as plan participants have more freedom of choice when investing pension assets.
  c. Need to provide increased transparency of up-to-date information.

Overall, the fundamental impacts to the Dutch pension system will remain to be seen as the DC plan is implemented in the next 4 years. While one waits to assess such impacts, it is clear that the system is moving to a decentralised structure with greater systemic transparency, personalisation, and security. Therefore, it is prudent that as a result of the changing nature of pension plans in the Netherlands a solution that has these characteristics is the clear answer as it would resolve the potential downfalls such a system could pose.

4.2.2 The Solution: APG & PGGM

Within the landscape of pension providers in the Netherlands, there is currently a Blockchain based solution that is being developed by firms APG and PGGM. While this solution has been/is being developed independently from the most recent legal changes to the pension system, it is important to assess as it will inadvertently resolve many of the concerns the Wtp will bring. As identified, the Wtp will bring about the need for mass data transparency that is up to date at any given point within a highly secure framework.

APG and PGGM have structured a DLT (more specifically a blockchain) solution that targets many of the sub areas of the new problems one could potentially see in the pension system. APG and PGGM have partnered to create a pension solution that is based on blockchain technology, where each of the 'blocks' is representative of a moment in a person's life (AiCIO, 2017). As the blockchain is capturing every life moment, it is readily accessible/auditable/reportable to all parties that are participants in the pension system. This would include the authorities, the pension fund, the pension supervisor and whoever else is needed to have data accessibility. Additionally, such a solution would be transparent and provide a complete overview of the full pensions with a breakdown of how that pension status was reached. As there is a need for mass amounts of information at any given time, the APG and PGGM solution seems like a natural fit as it also provides the necessary security (blockchain technology) if implemented properly to supervise a widescale pension system that is ready for the world of tomorrow.

The proposition by APG and PGGM is important as it could positively contribute to the wider issues that exist already and issues that may arise with the introduction of Wtp. With this proposition, the two providers should look to analyse how the relation of structures and technology will be important in such an implementation. The key missing element in the press releases and preliminary information available is that the persons that engage with these structures will be responding to the Wtp and if assumptions on a solution are based on today's scenario prior to implementation they may be faulty. The reason is due to reflexive monitoring, as suggested by Gidden, where the individuals will actively reshape structures through their interactions as a response to changes in said structures. Both the pension holders may react as well as regulators and administrators which impacts how the system operates. Due to this the STS concept of joint optimisation is further important as each structure is only as good as the use of it and jointly social, technical elements need to be optimised for ideal performance. This end result is a benefit to everyone which interacts in the system and not only the individual; however, it is extremely important to look at the engagement of a pension system also from an individual's perspective and therefore we look to such a case scenario.

4.3 Case Study: Process of Transferring a Pension

In order to get a direct insight into the process of transferring a pension, we had the opportunity to monitor this process first person. This process highlighted how even a straightforward pension transfer requires several weeks to progress due to inefficient infrastructure and processes.

The full history of correspondence during the transfer process can be found in Appendix 1.

Fig. 4.1 below provides a high-level timeline for the (incomplete) transfer process:

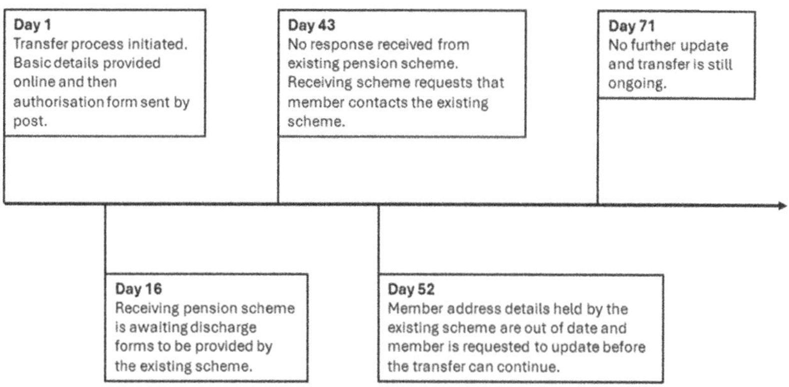

Fig. 4.1 Pension Transfer Lead Time Overview

Although this transfer did not complete in the timeframe that we had to complete the case study, we were able to gain a number of important insights into the pension transfer process.

In most cases it is not possible to transfer investments between pension plans, but instead liquidate the investments, transfer cash and then reinvest the cash once it is at the receiving pension fund. This means that the pension is not invested during the transfer process.

If the process runs smoothly, then a cash transfer as described above is expected to take 2–4 weeks. If it is possible to transfer investments directly then the process is expected to take 6–8 weeks. During this period, it will not be possible to make changes to investments.

The process cannot be completed online and requires multiple documents to be physically signed and posted, which is inefficient and increases the timeline.

There needs to be close communication between the receiving pension plan and the existing plan. There is no agreed service level agreement between the different pension plans and the transfer cannot progress whilst responses are outstanding. In our case study there was a delay of 6 weeks whilst the receiving pension plan waited for a response from the existing pension plan. The proposed solution was that the member should contact the existing plan themselves to 'give them a nudge'.

If the member has forgotten to update personal details with one of the pension providers, then any inconsistencies will further delay the process. In our case study, this caused further delay as the two plans were holding inconsistent address information for the member.

At the end of our 10-week case study, the transfer was not complete.

4.4 Case Study: IRM, Multi-Country pensions and the Current Landscape

While we looked to a specific individual scenario in engagement of the pension systems, we need to also take a wider look to the landscape that is impacting the consideration for both pension systems and pension processing. It is clear that there is an identified link between stakeholders and the structures; wherever there is a large shifting stress on a structure it is important to look at the relationship of how it is shifting and thus we look to a multi-country understanding and migration landscape. This is especially true in understanding Time-Space Distanciation, as we expect for social systems to become lesser and lesser varied as the cross-communication increases; as a result of this, it is important to study the global context of pension systems to truly understand if there is necessity in assessing from a singular country basis only or if multi-country pension systems are also relevant as a topic of study—a point which is further supported by STS theory as engagement with the structures needs to be assessed based on the Structure, Task, Technology and People interactions that exist. Therefore, we look to conceptualise the multi-country viewpoint.

According to the Global Migration Database from the United Nations, as of 2020 there were 281 million persons that resided in a country other than their country of birth (United Nations—Population Division, 2020). Almost 3 out of 4 of these migrants were between the ages of 20 to 64 (approximately 210 million). There are many causes for global migration (economic migrants, human rights migration, climate migration), however it is important to note that most of these migrants are at least several years into their working age.

There is an extremely important subset of migrants which are moving across countries and initiating contributions into several pensions systems or moving as part of what has been dubbed "International Retirement Migration" (IRM). While the latter is a small subset relative to the 210 million, it has been documented as a growing trend since the 1970 s (Savas et al, 2023).

The main mention of countries that supply to the trend are the United Kingdom, the USA, Germany, The Netherlands, and Sweden. Between these countries they contribute 8 million pensioners living abroad from their home country and there are trend indications that this will only continue to grow. Before looking to the statistics, we need to note a limitation; the information was pulled as an initial reference from the Global Migration Database and further leveraged from the specific country sites on tracking of pensioners' abroad. This means that the data is pulled by different year from each country; however, this is not as important as the relative example remains consistent since the number of new pensioners' abroad is at current of negligible amount to the overall population. As a result, we then look to break down these statistics and the following table indicates the current landscape of pensioners living abroad from their countries of origin:

The reason for looking at the top 5 mentioned countries rather than the volume indicators is twofold:

1. These countries have indicated this is statistically significant for pension considerations and important in policy discussions.
2. There is a lack of availability to cross-compare statistics, especially with countries that do not have this phenomenon recorded.

Table 4.2 Pensioners Living Abroad in Top 5 Country Mentions

Country of Origin	Total Amount of Pensioners Abroad (estimates)	Additional Notes
USA	5 million	1 in 6 pensioners is estimated, note that .8 million payout directly into a non-US account (Currency Fair, 2023; Adamczyk, 2024)
Germany	1.4 million	1/3 higher than previous years, there are no official statistics and we need to rely on estimates from *Deutsche Rentenversicherung* that 7% of 20 million German pensioners live abroad (Logan, 2023; Deutsche Rentenversicherung, 2024);
United Kingdom	1.1 million	Growing in recent years (Shabani, 2023; Emery, 2024)
Netherlands	0.6 million	1 in 11 pensioners live abroad (Centraal Buereau voor de Statistiek, 2007)
Sweden	0.2 million	Projected to be 0.8 million in 45 years (Regeringskansliet, 2020)

In addition to the above, it is important to mention that while this phenomenon of International Retirement Migration is generally viewed as an occurrence in the West it has become more widespread and is especially experiencing growth in Asia. One such example is with Japanese pensioners moving abroad at higher rates and even local governments, such as Malaysia, trying to attract these retirees (Immigration Department of Malaysia—Ministry of Home Affairs, 2024).

Notably, with the impacts of the COVID-19 pandemic it remains to be seen what exact implications exist with cross-border migration post-retirement and impact of nomadic digitalism deeper into the 21st century. One is able to expect that the natural trend is a further increase in globalised retirement migration well into the next 50 years and into the closure of the century.

4.4.1 The Application of Cross-border Agreements and Laws

The flow of migration is challenging to fully track within certain degrees of confidence. Even more so it is difficult for both governing bodies and individuals to ensure the pensioners remain compliant with home country and host country pension requirements if they plan on retiring and withdrawing from both systems. In some cases, Double Taxation Treaties, International Social Security Agreements (or otherwise known as Totalization agreements) exist between countries to aid in such cases. These agreements are generally bilateral and written for many purposes including: to mitigate risks to an individual for working on short term assignments for a multi-national corporation (dual coverage problem), facilitate social security comparisons between countries, breakdown the requirements for retirees, elucidate applications for benefits and claims for benefits (The United States Social Security Administration, 2024).

While agreements or guidance exists in cases where there are bilateral agreements or multilateral agreements (European Union), there are simply no such agreements for other countries. For example, if one looks to *Table 4.2* above and takes the country with the most pensioners living abroad; this country, the USA, only has 68 valid Double Taxation Treaties and 30 totalization agreements (The United States Social Security Administration, 2024). As a pensioner, it is extremely difficult to track on a consistent basis if there is a change in validity to the agreements, what the regulations are in both countries and data for what they may be entitled to depending on where they have worked previously. On the other hand, as a regulating entity (e.g. governments) it is difficult to have full transparency on the retirees and the amounts that they are receiving that could be potentially taxable in the host country. As a results for both the pensioners and the governments, it is increasingly complicated to track all of the information that is flowing through different systems both effectively and efficiently. As a result, there are law firms that specialise in offering guidance specifically for pensioners that are planning to retire abroad and even then much of the responsibility lays on the pensioners shoulders as they need to ensure compliance over the remaining time with their pension payouts.

4.4.2 A Specific Example in Retiring Abroad

While the above demonstrates a theoretical need based on generalised statistics and information that is readily available, it does not showcase the practical result of specific scenarios and requirements that are required for an individual to assess on a personal level what is required. As such, we propose a look into 3 individuals that we identify as Individuals A, B and C to illustrate the impact of different country constellations and the variance in difficulty to have a standard set of assessments for each (where the home country was chosen as the USA to give a control for the individuals) (Table 4.3):

Table 4.3 Assessment of Home/Host Country Taxation Agreements

Individual	Home Country	Host Country	Double Taxation Agreement	Totalization Agreement	Complexity
Individual A	USA	United Kingdom	Yes	Yes	Low
Individual B	USA	Turkey	Yes	No	Medium
Individual C	USA	Croatia	No	No	High

Looking to Individual A and B, they both have a Double Taxation agreement which provides a legal basis for tax protections to ensure they are not double taxed; however, only the United Kingdom, as the host country, has a Social Security Agreement (Totalization) which covers the individual. Individual C will have to navigate both systems entirely on their own in consolidation of the pension plans and attempt to keep themselves whole in retirement to ensure they are not subject to undue taxation. The table clearly showcases the increasing complexity as you run down the table and does not even consider multiple country destinations that the individuals may have worked.

As part of this process, we additionally ran a survey collection to understand which scenarios could be applicable. As aforementioned, the response pool was small (n = 20) and anonymous, however it remains imperative to the research we are engaging in. In the respondent's pool, about half had worked abroad with most working more than 1 year which means that they were taxable and contributed to the host countries pension pools. More interestingly, a quarter of the survey respondents planned to retire in countries other than their own and indicated countries which do not have Totalization agreements between their main home country and those they worked in. Overall, with the respondent's pool we noticed similarities and parallels to the main countries listed above in Table 4.1 for where pensioners live abroad.

We sought to understand how large the cross-country pension landscape is and whether this landscape is sufficient to target, in considering a solution, due to the population size or whether it is not sufficient enough as a main group. The main finding is that although the population of migrants with applicable cross country pension scenarios is in several hundred millions, the number of pensioners globally is almost 1 billion of which the ones' remaining in their home countries are a larger set (International Labour Organization, 2024; World Bank Group, 2023). In acknowledging this finding, we should also take note that the population of migrants that is traveling cross-country has only grown as have those that engage with global systems and structures rather than just local ones. As aforementioned, Gidden's emphasises this with Time-Space Distanciation and as a result, we see that there is a growing migratory population which needs to be tracked as it will have impacts in the future on local, regional and global systems; however, for the needs of a proposition in the pension space the multi-country population is niche and rather the target should remain a singular approach (which overtime may be considered across countries).

4.5 Expert Interviews

In order to better understand how pension plans operate and the challenges that they face, we undertook expert interviews with key stakeholders in the pension ecosystem (for further information on the findings in the interview please go to the appendix). We selected these interviewees based on quality rather than quantity. Firstly, it is difficult to find direct experts for a newly emerging and developing field and secondly, quality is paramount to truly understanding the depth of issues and challenges faced within the pension field among many stakeholders. As a result, we focused on top management in companies which allowed us to inquire directly on the state of the systems, stakeholders, main areas of concern and relevance of potential solutions to the field (Table 4.4).

From the figure above, it is very clear that the experts participating in the interview are all valuable sources of information even though they are coming from different fields of practice. They each hold vital information through which we can view the current pension and strategic solution landscape; both in viewing the field of information similarly or also differently to draw diverse conclusions about the space.

It is important to identify interview similarities among the experts. We found especially a clear comparison between all three in the mention of inefficiencies in the current system. The interviewees all mentioned that in transactions being

Table 4.4 List of Expert Interviews Conducted

Date	Job Title	Company	Location
26th April 2024	Director of Strategic Initiatives	Leading occupational pensions administrator	Ireland
2nd May 2024	Director of M&A Pension & Benefits	Fortune 100 company	Germany
7th May 2024	Global Product Manager Digital Assets, Managing Director	Global custody bank	USA

made (assets transferred, systemic updates, transaction solutions) therein lies the inefficiency of the current system and it is imperative that any solutions made surrounding the space identify such inefficiencies. The Global Product Manager of Digital Assets went further to mention that there needs to be a key distinction in this solution to the inefficiencies that exist; a distinction between a "data solution" and a "transaction solution." In other words, a data solution will aggregate and distribute information while transaction solutions will process transactions. Moreover, another similarity was tied to the general speed or expectation in which a solution could be rolled out. All three of the interviews made mention to the regulated landscape and risk averse nature of the pension field. The Director of M&A Pension and Benefits and the Global Product Manager of Digital Assets both elaborated on their points much further. The former indicated that large companies tend to run extremely risk-averse strategies when it comes to further developments of technology or adoption of technology that is still perceived to be experimental while the latter looked at this from the regulatory landscape indicating that activities in this area are highly controlled and measured leading to any potential proof of concept implementations being limited or slowed.

Through each of the interviewees we also had a different lens of approach to the subject matter which we need to take additional advantage of when we consider potential solutions in the pensions space and considerations that the experts identified as relevant. As such we have identified the key features of the interviews to ensure clear conclusions which can be utilised to create a framework of understanding of the key insights in the pension field and potential solutions.

The first interview with the Director of Strategic Initiatives validated our understanding of the relevant pension structure setup within one of our case studies of the UK pension system. Further, they verified how the systemic structure is setup in the background of the front facing system by identifying detailed items. This drove a deeper understanding into the methodology of agreements that are created in the UK occupational pension space (trust-based, contract-based) which led to the investment of pension assets and preparation for retirement. What is core to the discussion was that the members of the plans do not own the underlying funds, and these are instead held by the Trustee (trust-based) or pension provider (contract-based) which retain a register of the assets for each member. When the funds are in need to be transferred, then the members mentioned need to be liquidated before cash is transferred for re-investment into a new plan. This results in high maintenance efforts for the registers which dissect the share of assets per members; even the interviewee here indicated that this is challenging not only on the transaction level but that the plans will want to ensure that their assets are invested throughout the process (buy/sell is executed by sending/receiving providers). Throughout the interview there was high emphasis placed on the use of a balance sheet and registers to record the transactions.

The second interview with the Director of M&A Pension & Benefits at a Fortune 100 company helped to elucidate the corporate aspect of thought and administrative provision of pensions to the employees (members). While the interviewee themselves was not familiar of potential blockchain or DLT implementations in the field, several comments were made in regard to potential issues and solutions to the space which would be a necessary driver for any solutions in the space. The corporate space, according to the Director, is risk-averse which results in a general approach of caution when new developments are coming into the space; however, this carefulness should not be replaced with inaction. The benefit of a future solution needs to outweigh the potential risks and such a solution should focus on the transaction not in the storing of the information for accessibility. The true benefit is in creating an efficiency with a trusted technology and the Director further elaborates to mention whether a cloud-based solution could be just as effective as a DLT based solution. The key mention was that, by now, cloud-based solutions are quite regularly involved in the corporate context and the applicability could be easier to be described and approached than a DLT solution due to the underlying knowledge of the systems. One of the main takeaways throughout the interview is that the solution (regardless of whether Cloud, DLT or other) needs to be flexible and that "Pension solutions are paramount to benefits provision and the employee lifecycle", meaning that a system needs to be considered through the lens of the employee not only through the lens of the corporate or the regulator.

The third and final interview we conducted was with a Global Product Manager Digital Assets, Managing Director at a global custody bank. In this interview we deepened our understanding of the role of transfer agents and how efficiencies in this space would be achieved through the use of a potential DLT solution. What is noteworthy is that the Managing Director was the first of the interviewees to indicate that within their space there already was direct research into DLT and directly commented on this that the bank believes "DLT and smart contracts will improve operational processes, whilst ensuring security and accuracy". Furthermore, a cross-functional Digital Assets Working Group has been formed and is focused on targeted proof of concepts. This is incredibly valuable as it introduces the validity of a DLT solution in the role of a transfer agent which can be more specifically narrowed to a transfer agent in pension administration. Additionally, the "peak-behind the curtain" of a transfer agent supported our notion that the process is extremely burdened by manual processes: faxes, emails and telephone calls are all prevalent in the transfer agent activities.

Overall, the interviews reconfirmed the need for a solution in the pension ecosystem and when coupled with the case studies reviewed, as well as supplemental research, the direction becomes clear that a technological solution needs to be found for the pension system to remain a functional part in society for the near future.

5 Results & Recommendations

The UK and Netherlands case studies are a clear demonstration of the challenges that many countries are facing to ensure adequate pensions savings for their residents, and the innovative solutions that they are implementing. However, it is also clear that these solutions are introducing new challenges that existing infrastructure is unable to address.

The UK 'Auto Enrolment' programme has increased pension participation rates to 88% but this has had the side effect of creating many small pension pots distributed across a number of pension providers/administrators. This creates a challenge for the pension holder to track their pension assets and also for the pension provider due to the costs of administering many small pots held my many different individuals. Specifically, there are an estimated 12 million pension pots below £1,000 with total assets of £4.2 billion. Whilst the aggregate sum is vast, the individual pots are worth an average of £350. It is not viable to manage pension pots of this size and the administration costs will quickly erode the value of these.

B. Terzic and N. King, *A DLT Solution for Efficient Large-Scale Pension Administration*, BestMasters, https://doi.org/10.1007/978-3-658-48591-7_5

The UK government has consulted on a number of solutions to this problem and in implementing a consolidation approach to roll up these small pensions into manageable pots. A key requirement of this solution is 'having a central point or system to manage and match data' and it is proposed that this could be achieved by either a central clearing house or central registry. The preferred solution is a clearing house approach due to simplicity for pension providers connecting with a single centralised organisation. However, concerns have been raised regarding how this approach would be funded to develop the required infrastructure and systems. Interestingly, a DLT solution was not mentioned, even though this would seem to achieve the best of both proposed solutions of the clearing house and registry. The potential of a new technology to help achieve each of these possible solutions is quite clear. They require sensitive personal data to be shared amongst multiple parties in a secure and efficient way.

The Dutch government is facing similar demographic challenges which are causing a strain on what was historically a primarily DB-based pension system. This case study has highlighted the benefits and challenges of a move from a DB to DC system to the key stakeholders involved—individuals, corporates (employers) and pension plan providers. It is clear that there are a number of benefits to employers as they are transferring investment risk to the pension holders and potentially reducing costs. However, there is also a cost of implementing this for the employer and even more so for pension providers. The technology solution needs to ensure that separate pots individually manged by pension holders can be easily administered and provide easy access to up-to-date information. APG and PGGM, two of the largest pension providers in the Netherlands have partnered to create a blockchain based solution which they look to adapt for this.

Our next case study demonstrates the experience of an individual seeking to transfer a pension pot from one pension platform to another. It is quite clear that the current infrastructure and technology used by pension administrators is very inefficient. If the process goes smoothly, then it is expected to take several weeks and is likely to result in the pension holder being out of the market for a significant period of time, impacting investment returns. In our case study the process was far from smooth, requiring forms to be physically sent by mail, then delays waiting for responses from the pension administrators. Inconsistent personal information recorded by the different administrators then blocked any further progress. The transfer was still incomplete at the end of our 10-week case study.

If the different administrators were operating on a common open infrastructure, then this would simplify the process significantly, allowing for consistent information to be maintained and exchanged instantaneously. A potential solution would need to allow this to happen securely with full auditability. This is likely to result in a far better experience for the pension holder and also reduce costs for the administrators.

This case study highlights the inefficiency of transferring one pension pot for one individual with significant effort required from the pension holder and the administrator. As mentioned in the UK case study, there are 20 million of these pots worth less than £10,000.

These first three case studies demonstrate some of the complexities of evolving pensions systems within individual countries. Taking this one step further, we then look at individuals that have worked in multiple countries throughout their career accruing pension pots in multiple countries. This now introduces additional dimensions of complexity as there will be additional tax implications when the individual retires. This will require accurate, transparent information at an aggregate level, providing further support for a solution which can address these aspects.

In order to better understand the infrastructure that is currently being used in pension administration, we conducted interviews with:

- Director within one of the largest pension administration platforms serving the UK and Europe.
- A Managing Director within a global custody bank which provides custody and transfer agency services.

These experts were able to provide a clear view of the different stakeholders and roles involved in pensions administration. Based on the discussions, in Figs. 3.1 and 3.2 below we have adapted the pension participant mapping from Sarker and Datta to show the roles of each participant and the relationship between participants in trust-based and contract-based plans in the UK. Whilst we have focused on the UK market for this interview, the structure is generally representative across markets (Figs. 5.1 and 5.2).

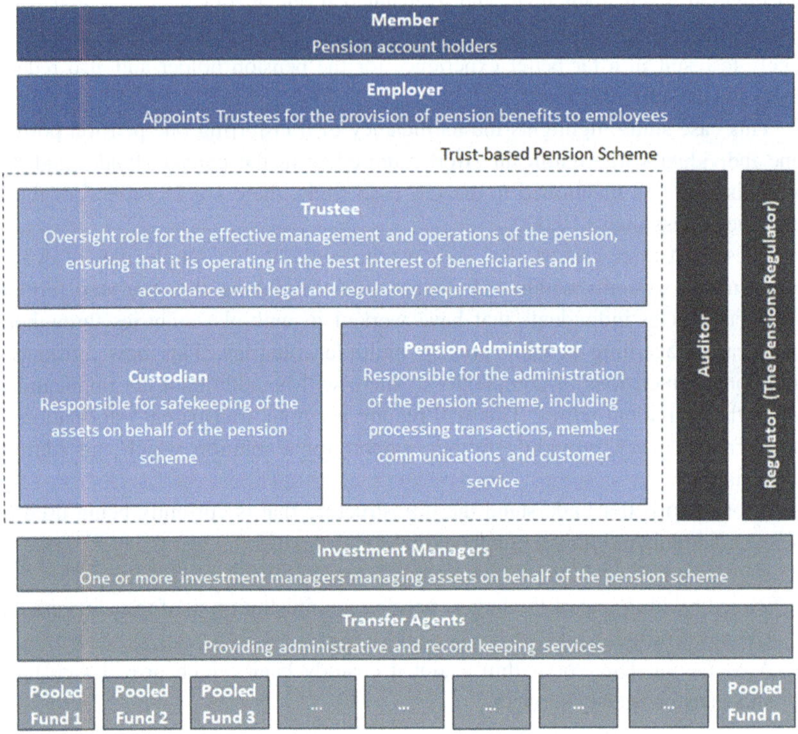

Fig. 5.1 Major participants in a trust-based pension plan (UK example)

It is clear from these charts that there are multiple participants which play an important role in supporting pension plans. Sensitive financial data needs to be carefully stored and transferred between these participants. The contract-based plan is a simpler structure as the member is able to engage directly with the plan via the pension platform provider.

The pooled funds depicted at the bottom of the charts are investment vehicles where assets of several pension plans may be comingled. Transfer agents (TAs) provide an important administrative role here, recording the share of the fund held by each pension plan. They also process subscription and redemption transactions within the funds. The transfer agency services may be provided by the investment manager or another third party (often a custody bank).

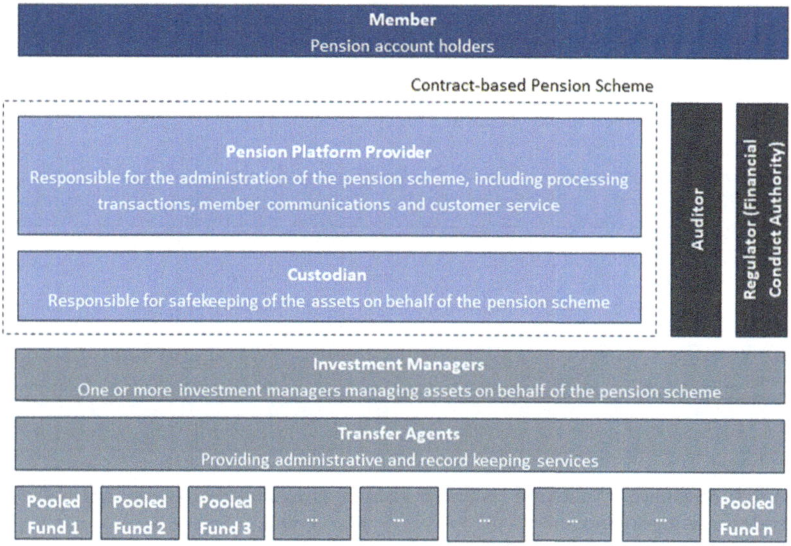

Fig. 5.2 Major participants in a contract-based pension plan (UK example)

The investment manager then invests these assets according to the investment objective and policy of the fund. The assets will be held securely by in safe custody by a bank, which is a highly regulated activity.

A pension platform or administrator will handle transactions and communications with the individual pension holders. Similar to the TA role described above, the pension administrator will record the share of assets held by each member.

There are two levels of ledger information being stored:

- The TA records holdings of each pension plan in each of the pooled funds.
- The pension platform/administrator records allocation of the pension plans members.

This relationship is shown in Fig. 4.1 below. Note that a transfer agent can act on behalf of multiple funds (Fig. 5.3).

There will be many pension providers (PPs) in a particular market, and each will generally have multiple TA relationships as set out on Fig. 5.1 below. Note

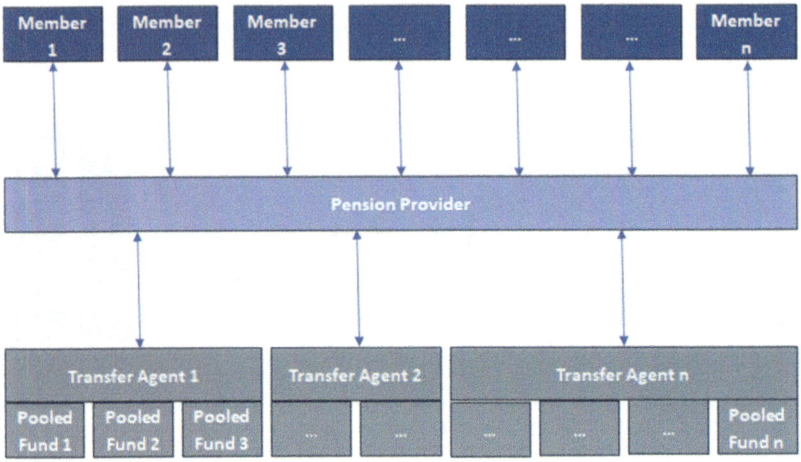

Fig. 5.3 Simplified relationship between pension provider/administrator, pension plan members and transfer agents.

that funds might be exclusively available for a particular PP or available to multiple PPs (Fig. 5.4).

To complicate matters further, an individual may have multiple pensions with multiple PPs, accessing a range of different funds. This could happen has they move jobs and have a new pension with each employer. This is set out in Fig. 5.2 below (Fig. 5.5).

In the examples that follow, we will assume that the individual has the following pensions:

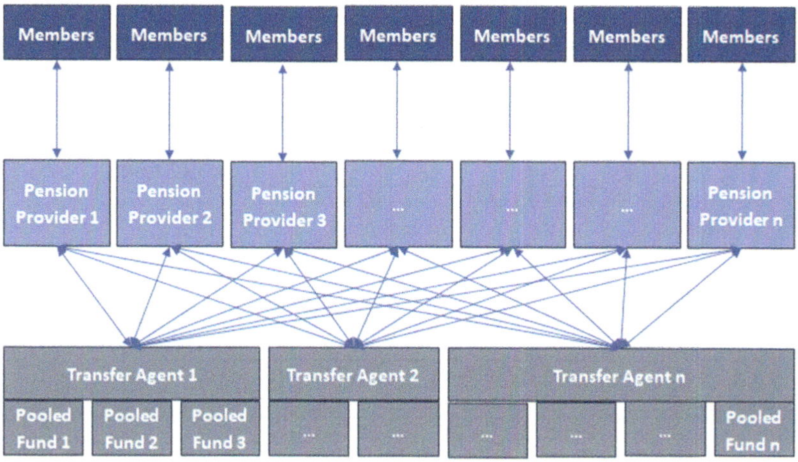

Fig. 5.4 Pension providers will have multiple TA relationships to access the funds on behalf of their members.

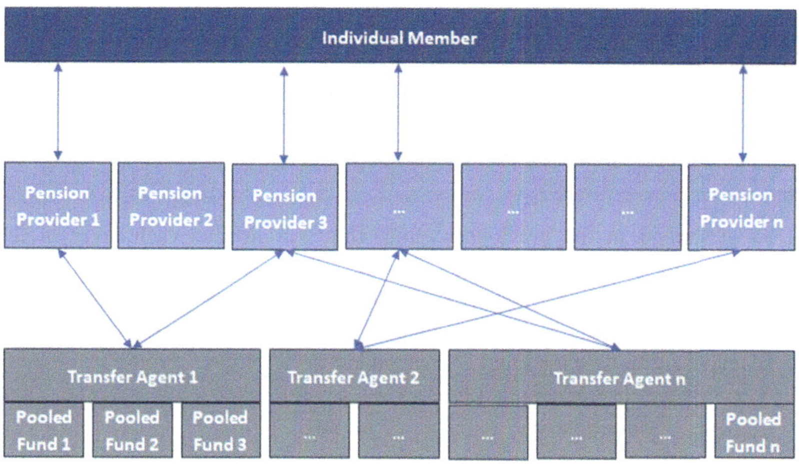

Fig. 5.5 An individual may have multiple pensions with different providers

Pension Provider	Fund	Value	Total Value per Pension Provider
Pension Provider 1	Fund 1 (TA 1)	€10,245	€31,986
	Fund 3 (TA 1)	€21,741	
Pension Provider 3	Fund 2 (TA 1)	€9,745	€22,201
	Fund 3 (TA 1)	€3,333	
	Fund 105 (TA n)	€8,123	
Pension Provider 4	Fund 33 (TA 2)	€5,741	€16,049
	Fund 38 (TA 2)	€6,951	
	Fund 123 (TA n)	€3,357	
Pension Provider n	Fund 33 (TA 2)	€7,154	€14.370
	Fund 46 (TA 2)	€1,743	
	Fund 50 (TA 2)	€5,473	

As described in the previous section, this will involve each layer in the structure maintaining separate ledgers to represent these holdings.

Each fund will have its own separate ledger, representing the holdings of each PP. This register will be maintained by the TA that is servicing the fund.

Example of register for Fund 2 (maintained by TA 1):

Beneficiary	Amount
PP 3	€333,621,785
PP n	€111,419,113
...	

Example of register for Fund 3 (maintained by TA 1):

Beneficiary	Amount
PP 1	€246,005,123
PP 3	€15,125,251
...	

Each PP will then have a ledger which representing how its holdings in each fund are allocated across the various members.

Example of register maintained by PP 3:

Fund	Beneficiary	Value	Total Value of holdings in this fund
Fund 2	Our example member	€9,745	€333,621,785
	Another member	€xxx	
	...	...	
Fund 3	Our example member	€3,333	€15,125,251
	Another member	€xxx	
	...		
Fund 105	Our example member	€8,123	€9,644,816
	Another member	€xxx	
	...		
...	...	...	...

One challenge that the individual will have is with seeing their aggregate level of assets across PPs. Each PP will show the value of the funds held with them but there is not usually an easy way to see total pensions savings and how these are allocated. The UK Pensions Dashboard Programme is designed to address this issue.

A more significant issue is the complexity involved if the individual decides to consolidate these pensions. As an example, we will look at consolidating PP 3 into PP 1. As we have seen in case study 3, this involves the following steps:

(1) Member contacts PP 1 to advise them of intention to transfer assets from PP 3.
(2) PP 1 will then contact PP 3, requesting that they initiate a transfer.
(3) Depending on the Pension Providers, the transfer may happen as cash (more usual) or it may be possible to transfer the holdings in the individual funds.

5.1 Cash Pension Transfer

If the transfer happens as cash, then PP 3 will contact TA 1 to redeem €9,745 in Fund 2 and €3,333 in Fund 3. PP 3 will also contact TA n to redeem €3,357 in Fund 105. TA 1 and TA 3 will update their registers to reflect the reduced holdings of PP 3. Corresponding, PP 3 will update its register to reflect the reduced fund holdings of the member. Once the cash proceeds from the redemptions are received by PP 3, this will be transferred to PP 1 and the transfer is complete.

The ledger/account entries for these transactions are shown below. To simplify the example, we have not shown the accounts of the Funds which would reflect sale of underlying securities and cash in to pay the redemption proceeds.

Fund 2 register (maintained by TA 1) will be updated as follows:

Beneficiary	Amount
PP 3	(€9,745)

Fund 3 register (maintained by TA 1) will be updated as follows:

Beneficiary	Amount
PP 3	(€3,333)

Fund 105 register (maintained by TA N) will be updated as follows:

Beneficiary	Amount
PP 3	(€8,123)

PP 3 register will be updated as follows:

Fund	Beneficiary	Amount
Fund 2	Our example member	(€9,745)
Fund 3	Our example member	(€3,333)
Fund 105	Our example member	(€8,123)

PP 3 cash account will be updated as follows:

Source	Beneficiary	Fund	Amount
Fund 2	Our example member	Cash In	€9,745
Fund 3	Our example member	Cash In	€3,333
Fund 105	Our example member	Cash In	€8,123
Our example member	PP 1	Cash Transfer Out	(€22,201)

PP 1 cash account will be updated as follows:

Source	Beneficiary	Fund	Amount
PP 3	Our example member	Cash Transfer In	€22,201

The member will now have €22,201 cash in their PP 1 account which will need to be invested in the relevant funds.

5.2 Fund Unit Pension Transfer

If the transfer happens by moving the fund units, then PP 3 will contact the TAs to request transfer of the relevant fund holdings to PP 3. This is not generally straight forward. For example, as we can see in Fig. 5.2, PP 1 does not have an account with TA n, therefore it is not possible to move the units in Fund 105 and this will need to happen as cash. There will also be other operational constraints that mean that a unit transfer is often not possible or is very time consuming.

For this simplified example, we will assume that all funds are available to all PPs as long as they have the relevant TA relationship. In reality, this may not be the case. TA 1 will update its register reducing the positions held by PP 3 in Fund 2 and Fund 3 and correspondingly increasing the positions held by PP 1.

Fund 2 register (maintained by TA 1) will be updated as follows:

Beneficiary	Amount
PP 3	(€9,745)
PP 1	€9,745

Fund 3 register (maintained by TA 1) will be updated as follows:

Beneficiary	Amount
PP 3	(€3,333)
PP 1	€3,333

Fund 105 register (maintained by TA N) will be updated as follows:

Beneficiary	Amount
PP 3	(€8,123)

PP 3 register will be updated as follows:

Fund	Beneficiary	Amount
Fund 2	Our example member	(€9,745)
Fund 3	Our example member	(€3,333)
Fund 105	Our example member	(€8,123)

PP 3 cash account will be updated as follows:

Source	Beneficiary	Fund	Amount
Fund 105	Our example member	Cash In	€8,123
Our example member	PP 1	Cash Transfer Out	(€8,123)

PP 1 register will be updated as follows:

Fund 2	Beneficiary	Amount
Fund 2	Our example member	€9,745
Fund 3	Our example member	€3,333

PP 1 cash account will be updated as follows:

Source	Beneficiary	Fund	Amount
PP 3	Our example member	Cash Transfer In	€8,123

The member will now have €8,123 cash in their PP 1 account which will need to be invested in the relevant funds.

These simplified examples show that the transfer agents and pension administrators are each operating separate closed ledgers which requires communications to coordinate and reconcile. This causes costly and unnecessary administration for the pension administrators and a poor experience for the pension holder due to the length transfer process.

6 Solution Conceptualisation

6.1 The Current System

"The art of simplicity is a puzzle of complexity"—Douglas Horton.

We established that pension systems suffer from such a puzzle of complexity that one must be able to look at the current landscape through both a magnifying glass on one eye and on the other a telescope to ensure that the mitigation of risk currently done by the systems can be transformed into an efficient landscape to the benefit of all within the system. It is important to note in the development of such a new system the system will always fall to the behest of regulatory requirements for the components within. Therefore, part of the focus on the system will be on creating one that is flexible and able to adjust in a manner befitting future regulation while continuing to ensure a critical role in ensuring financial security and societal welfare. The further focus will be the creation of a solution within a DC plan, as the primary and tertiary pillars are either in retrograde or growing at a much smaller pace in comparison the DC plans within the second pillar resulting in gaps of transparency, accessibility, and ease of understanding.

To reach a conclusion on a possible solution, one must first assess the evidence provided to us in the aforementioned sections of the current *Modus Operandi* of both the pension systems and those working within the landscape. As indicated in the expert interview with a Director of Strategic Initiatives and further research, the landscape consists of many actors including: the pension holders, employer, pension administrator, infrastructure provider, investment manager, regulator, credit bureau, financial intermediaries, and others. An overview of such a system is present in Fig. 3.1 to showcase the varying levels of complexity in only one segmentation of the pension system within the setup of a DC plan within the second pillar (in reviewing the figure it is important to keep in note that this is

B. Terzic and N. King, *A DLT Solution for Efficient Large-Scale Pension Administration*, BestMasters, https://doi.org/10.1007/978-3-658-48591-7_6

being replicated across a x number of corporates, y number of contributors that all need to be accounted for by regulatory bodies in any adjustment, change or shift no matter how minute).

In positioning a pension solution based on the above complexity, a few conclusions become certain. One of these is a DC based pension solution sits within enabling pension administration, custodian functions or being the solution to provide such services. The latter is more feasible as the local pension field is highly concentrated and the global field is difficult to enter due to complexity observed in the case studies (few global players, stronghold on the market). Another important conclusion is there are many inefficiencies presented in the above diagram as within each stakeholder transaction there is an intermediary that is handling the transaction and storage of information relevant at any given time in an extremely centralised manner without much transparency. This leads to a lengthy end-to-end execution timeframe which may run upwards of several business days to weeks in some scenarios. Due to the lengthy execution and many stakeholders the systemic data is constantly at risk and the security of the system is based on the obligation of each touchpoint in ensuring data security (some standards which may be locale based and not to the same standard as necessary across all systemic uses). To conclude, in between all of the intermediaries there are also several shifts or "life changes" that need to be accounted for succinctly in the pension system; at each job change, company shift the pension holder will be creating a pot creating another layer of complexity. A mathematical comparison would be that of a permutation (e.g. for a lock) where each order of selection matters and with each possibility it needs to be entered exactly as recorded to ensure a success; in the same manner, each of these new job changes needs to be recorded exactly in a subsequent manner to record the exact "combination" to the pension contributions (due to various limitations, statutes, regulations on the system). This example can be more exemplified within *Fig.* 5.1, which indicates that within one single transaction there are several intermediaries that need to be involved just to reflect (what seems to be) one single change for the pension holder due to a new investment strategy, a job change or life change. With each of these transactions the process becomes increasingly tedious as the average processing time is several business days for a change to be processed (as was identified first-hand through our case study).

Due to all the aforementioned conclusions, the burden of the current system is great and due to its inherent inability to scale will only continue to be greater while at the same time more data transparency, security and accessibility are needed.

The importance of this information is in understanding how complex a pension system can be, especially when considering multiple country factors. In general, even a single country pension system may run multiple complexities due to the three pillars generally prevalent in each country market; then taking this conceptually and looking at multi-country markets it raises the complexity substantially.

6.2 The Current Pension System, Leavitt's Diamond & Structuration Theory

The STS theory is built on 4 key elements and in order to assess the technology key element, one must understand the other 3 elements in their interdependency. As we assess the current pension system, it is also important to identify which topics are inherent to pension systems and which are subject to change in accordance with new regulations or adjustments in corporate policies. Additionally, we add a supplementary framework especially when it comes to understanding structure and the individual's relationship to structure.

6.2.1 Structure

The overall pension system has many different components which creates a complex mosaic of stakeholders, hierarchies, and interactions. Looking to the stakeholders we can see the following interacting in some extent with the pension systems:

1. Pension Holder—the employee (individual participant to the pension system)
2. Corporates—the employer
3. Government Authority (Public Pension System)—A pillar of the current system
4. Government Regulator—Ensuring fair provisioning and audit requirements are met
5. Pension Administrator—Provides the administration services enabling pensions
6. Pension Technology Platform—Provides the infrastructure for administration services
7. Platform Provider—Provide the infrastructure and administration services enabling pensions

8. Investment Manager—Ensure pension fund assets are managed in accordance with regulations and policies of the respective pension plan
9. Transfer Agency—Process and record transactions in funds, resulting in a ledger of holders of units in the funds
10. Credit Bureau/Credit Agency—checks on pension assets (indirect)
11. Financial Intermediaries (Banks, custodial banks)—safekeeping of pension assets

This list identifies a number of stakeholders involved or interacting with the pension system at any given time. The complexity of the structure of the pension system also increases when reviewing it from a lens of DC engagement. As we identified in the UK (and what is expected to be the case in the Netherlands), the increased usage of DC plans will increase the data touchpoints/interactions within each of the stakeholders. More importantly, each stakeholder will find greater necessity in documenting down to a further degree to ensure proper pension provision within the regulatory and policy framework.

What is important is to supplement the understanding of the stakeholders and look at this through the lens of Structuration theory. Individual agency seems quite limited when assessing the engagements in the system. This is however an incorrect assumption to make, while there are many stakeholders the individual has the most power in the system to exert influence to shape and reshape the system as the pension holder. This is identifiable through the demographics issues mentioned in the introductory section and must be kept as an important distinction in solutions considered.

6.2.2 Task & People

The pension system at its core (irrelevant of structure) aims to provide pensions for individuals involved in the system (most notably pension holders). The former is the task, in accordance with the STS model, and this defines what is the main goal of the system. With this definition, the core of our research needs to create an efficient provision for pensions and enhance the end-to-end output of such a system. This means that an efficient solution needs to administer, provide pensions (and transparency to stakeholders) with a short throughput to maximise the benefits to the structure of the system and the people. Furthermore, as the people are at the centre of such a system; the technology needs to be adaptable to provide the core pension holder ability for transparency while not hindering the constant motion of the pension system. We identified that in the case studies of today's pension system there are superfluous amounts of time spent with each intermediary and interaction of the system—either through a pension transfer request that takes upwards of two and a half months or a pension holder not being able to capture all of their pension provisions within a single source of truth.

Within the STS model there are interdependencies among the four key elements. As showcased above, structure, task and people are core in the decision-making process for which technological solution would make the pension system efficient.

Importantly, while the STS model indicates these interdependencies an additional one must be introduced here and that is the wider net of peoples engaging within the system. Specifically, the influence that is exerted and a special focus on the concept of Time-space distanciation as it drives core implications to just how adaptable the technology will need to be. With greater globalisation, more systems will be influenced by the exchange of persons which also results in further needs for the interaction of tasks and people to be better facilitated in a pension structure.

6.2.3 Leavitt's Diamond and Technology

The final key element in the STS model is technology. As there is a relation between the other three elements, we have identified that the main issues that arise from the current system are scalability, time efficiency, security, and data transparency. A modern solution would need to have the fortitude to provide encrypted data transfer and at the same time provide a layer coupled with data transparency and security. This is further bolstered by the need for a robust system capable of adaptability in a growing globalised environment.

In the search for potential solutions, we considered several different products or offerings which may be relevant. On-premise solutions were eliminated early on as they are singular in nature and localised which make data aggregation and management difficult over time as well as limited robustness of the solution (hence a natural transition away from on-premise solutions) (Kranz, Hanelt, & Kolbe, 2016). We want to ensure a movement forward in the pension technical landscape and when it comes to data issues, we need to ensure a forward movement rather than a parallel imitation of what is currently available.

In eliminating on premise solutions, we turn to research to understand the current landscape of pension systems. In assessing the landscape, we identified that the common adaptation in the pension field seems to be a general transition to increase in cloud service (away from on premise) use for Pension schemes in data aggregation, information storage and increasing accessibility for users (Al-Thobhani, 2017). Cloud systems offer great elasticity in data storage, use, and transformation as well as a distributed manner of accessing the information allowing for not only the flexibility of data but also system (Breit & Salomon, 2015). As a result, of the initial understanding cloud technology could offer the efficiency and versatility that could resolve the issues of modern pension systems introduced earlier in section 1. Before we continue to use cloud as a base solution, we need to define which cloud environment we are specifically focused on. There are two cloud-based solutions possible in the space:

1. Cloud solution as separated databases. All different stakeholders would have different entry points which need built interfaces between them to aggregate data or link data (usually through a data lake).
2. Cloud solution as a common database. Where a singular solution is used across all different stakeholders including administrators, transfer agents. Information is aggregated through use of a common platform.

The latter of the two cloud solutions is what we will utilise as our base definition. The reason for this is we want to assess future potential and not what is already widely available across the market. The first of the two solutions was a step from on-premise to cloud and the second of the two is an additional step for pension systems.

Furthermore, as we assessed the root issues plaguing or poised to plague pension plans, we look to propose a more novel solution: Distributed Ledger Technology (DLT). As analysed in the results and recommendations section we see that a core of issues lie in the complexity of the ledger calculations that need to occur. DLT is already being leveraged in other financial technology areas to resolve similar problems. Additionally, as we saw in the expert interviews, specific industry stakeholders have already set up teams to assess the applicability of the technology for wider applications. We naturally believe that DLT should be a part of the solution conversation for pension systems as the issues identified surrounding data, scalability, security and ledgers are central to other DLT solutions already implemented or in process of implementation.

In reviewing potential solutions, it is necessary to mention to the above potential candidates, a key distinguishing feature between the two potential solutions are the ledger capabilities of the systems. For DLT, this is system inherent and is key to why we consider this a potential solution for all of the issues currently on display within the pension system. For Cloud-based solutions it is not inherent, and commonly relies on additional system integrations. It is exactly due to these limitations that there is rudimentary research that has begun to identify potential mergers of cloud-based solutions and DLT technology to create a hybrid cloud, DLT-based platform (Stanke, Unterberg, Trauth, & Bergs, 2020; Westerlund & Kratzke, 2018; Trautmann, 2023); we have chosen to forego such a solution as there is not enough of a body of research and understanding as to how the technology would vary between each of the main solutions today: Cloud based or DLT based.

6.3 A Deeper Dive: Cloud Based Pension System

It is necessary to more deeply dive into Cloud technology in addition to the comparison above before a comparison can be undertaken between DLT and Cloud Technology. Cloud based technology is fairly new as a concept to the administration of pension systems and pension fund management. The technology has allowed for great technological strides in data aggregation, data transparency and can be seen as a necessary step to pave the way for future pension system overhauls. The system is flexible as it is able to be adjustable to the needed creation of infrastructure for pensions. The pension systems that leverage the technology have the potential for great versatility as data transparency can be toggled in the system, data is mutable to allow ease of following regulatory guidelines and is a scalable option based on the growth of data sets.

Cloud technology can bring about many needed positives to the pension space. From a technical standpoint, it has a quicker time to market than most solutions as new instances of the technology are able to be rolled out or retired within moments notice. This is extremely important when it comes to a space that has constant regulatory changes.

Further to this, the scalability and flexibility of cloud is rarely matched as the technology can be quickly scaled up to meet the necessary storage needs as well as scale down efficiently when these same resources are no longer needed. In the same direction as the time to market for cloud technology, scalability and flexibility are both important as there can be an (almost) immediate ramp up or ramp down of resources which leads to reduction of the technical gap that currently exists in current pension systems.

Another positive aspect of cloud technology is data accessibility, especially if it needs to be accessed worldwide as cloud technology is not device nor location specific. This is useful in scenarios where we assessed cross border movements of peoples and necessity for information usage to submit requests. Alongside accessibility, data loss prevention for cloud technology is a central benefit when backed up properly within the systems (although this can be questionable as we see in the critiques of the technology below).

The key areas in the cross-comparison above where we need to spend additional focus on are specifically the faults of the system as these bring about major concerns: centralisation risk, and security. The former, centralisation risk, is tied to the distribution of cloud platforms for business and consumer use. The major players, such as Google and AWS, provide cloud-based services which are centralised in the control of the provision. This can bring great risks and issues as while the company or user may have access; the control of the system remains with one party (the entity providing the infrastructure). This can cause especially odious issues akin to what occurred in Australia with a $125 billion pension fund being accidentally deleted (Taylor, 2024). This may also bring benefits in terms of legislation for an overseeing entity and ensuring enaction of strict guidelines; however, in this example the Australian Pension Fund had to oversee restoration of information from a previous backup which was outside of the Google ecosystem and a little over a year old. In the latter topic of security, it is developed for system usage. In most cases outside of corporate settings, Web 2.0 technology is leveraged (user, password, two-factor authentication in some cases). In these scenarios, as the data is stored in centralised servers and the entry points are based in Web 2.0 it needs a robust security cloud system to ensure integrity of the data and quickly control necessary hacks. This could be in cases of Denial-of-service attacks, poor network security or inadequate data encryption among other cases. The risks can be mitigated but never fully (and are only mitigated by higher expenditure on infrastructure).

There are weak points that need to be mentioned as part of what can be 'system inherent' in cloud-based systems: Data mutability, data transparency. Data transparency to the user can be limited which also impacts the accessibility. In general, cloud systems may logically segregate or create a separate instance of this information based on the ability to access the data. This can be a very good thing, however when it comes to getting data quickly and efficiently the system can be delayed depending on split reporting of environments or information (as before, there are opportunities to mitigate this, but it comes down to higher expenditure on infrastructure).

Moreover, data mutability can be mutable to a fault. This can be seen with what happened with the above-mentioned Australian pension fund, however it can also happen if there are not necessary checks inherently created within the system. Since the infrastructure tends to work on a centralised company/server basis, the data cannot be independently verified across the systems which lends itself to risk mitigation measures—which resolve the question of when it will occur and how likely, rather than if it will occur. Cloud-based systems are currently in process of implementation for many pension funds. However, we believe that these have inherent flaws and whilst they are step in the right direction, they are not a long-term solution for administration of outdated systems.

6.4 A Deeper Dive: DLT Based Pension System

The current available body of information indicates that a DLT solution is ideal as a technology based on the issues raised in modern pension systems. This does not mean that the technology is without fault, rather we have to fully understand whether it is the best suiting technology than currently available systems with bodies of theoretical and practical work surrounding it.

DLT solutions can bring scalability and decentralisation to implementations of the technology. As the technology is inherently based on a decentralised approach, this adds increased value due to distributed confirmations of the ledger which acts as a source of truth among the connected computers acting like nodes in the system. This potential use of decentralised (and single) ledger leads to potential improvements in the space also for the scalability of potential complexity that may arise in a single system. This is the core benefit in use of a DLT system; it has the capability to greatly reduce lead times in a process that may otherwise take *nth* times more to progress from start to finish.

As an additional benefit of scalability and decentralisation of the infrastructure, data accuracy, data aggregation and data security can be strengthened. The inherent property of decentralisation allows records to be added to the end of the ledger at any time but only to the end and that all nodes have a perpetual view of the ledger. This needs to be addressed in how the DLT system is established, however the potential for these data topics to be system inherent and coded allows for an extremely strong encryption of data that is decentralised—in other words, centralisation risk is low which also results in reduction of potential security breaches to a central system.

A final benefit to DLT is the accessibility of the data through connections that users can leverage to see their information in real-time. As the DLT is constantly running, real-time information is continuously provided which is extremely beneficial in the scenarios where the stakeholders could be users, regulatory bodies, or others which need access to the data in perpetuity to ensure processes, fund management and additional topics within the pension environment.

While from the above DLT appears to be well suited as a technological solution, it is not without its limits. Kuhn et al. note this in their paper identifying that a number of DLT solutions out there are in the blockchain sector which is at odds with requirements in many other application spaces (Rethinking Distributed Ledger Technology, 2019). When we look to a potential DLT solution for pensions, we need to carefully consider the pitfalls of a DLT system to ensure that these are either remedied in the solution or adopted as a calculated risk. In other words, the system may still function better than other solutions (and proposed solutions) in today's world; however, at a reasonable risk cost.

One clear example of this is the data mutability in the above comparison. In traditional DLT implementations, data immutability is championed. Though in the legal sphere and in accordance with law, data needs to be immutable as there could be changes/deletions that are often required to be possible. A clear substantiated instance of this is data privacy regulations across the globe and the necessity for data deletion requests to be followed. In a DLT model when it comes to the public sphere of usage in a highly regulated sector, we need to ensure that the technology does not follow suite with its more publicised implementation alongside blockchain—as this will then create systemic issues of regulation and legal coherence.

A further example of a risk which is also applicable here is considering a consensus model or mechanism for the potential DLT solution. As the ledger is distributed within the system, how the system is updated across the ledgers (e.g. within each of the nodes) is important to consider especially as there is a core criticism that lies here. Depending on the consensus mechanism, these generally tend to draw heavy burdens on power and infrastructure surrounding the system especially as the indicated aim above is to create a system that is more efficient in processing and providing data at any given moment.

Overall, when looking at the given the risks and potential pitfalls of a DLT based solution we need to understand how to truly leverage the full capability of DLT. We will need to assess how to structure a solution that will work the best for key areas in the pension system and bring about the most recent technological revolutions into a dated space in cross comparing other cloud-based solutions.

6.5 Comparing the Two: Cloud & DLT

As mentioned by the Director of M&A Pension Systems and Benefits: if a DLT solution is proposed why would not a cloud-based solution be possible in its stead and potentially better? The answer to this is very simple, both are feasible solutions; however, we need to engage in a more thorough analysis to identify which would actually bring about better systemic influence and change long term. Also, we need to assess which will be inherently more inclined to solving the problems of the current pension system.

In a general review of the two potential solutions, the Cloud based solution leaves openings that are not inherent in being solved by the system such as security issues, cost management and lack of resources. For DLT, the solutions for any issues are inherently solved by the system rather than outside circumstances that would need to be mitigated. DLT does offer inherent solution characteristics and it is possible for a cloud-based solution to reach the same efficiency as a DLT solution, however the solutions are not innate to the system architecture like security and scalability are to a DLT solution. A DLT solution will need a basis of resources, however it becomes less resources intensive when scaling up due to the inherent nature of the ledger technology.

The best scenario for a cross-comparison between the two would be to assess on a one-to-one basis the efficacy of the systems across several paradigms that would be required for the running of a DC plan within the second pillar (Table 6.1):

Table 6.1 Cross Comparison of a Cloud Based and DLT based solution

Solution	Cloud Based Solution	DLT Solution
Accessibility	Limited, generally based on licenses	Open
Centralisation Risk	High	Low
Data Transparency	Can be system inherent	Yes, System inherent
Data Mutability	Can be system inherent	Generally low, can be made system inherent
Ledger	Not inherent, developed	Yes, System inherent
Scalability	Yes	Yes
Security	Not inherent, developed	Yes, System inherent

As a result of the above analysis, a cloud-based solution can be made to behave more like a DLT solution to solve the issues. This lends us to an assumed notion that the DLT solution would be a better approach as the system inherently resolves flaws that would arise with a developed cloud solution. Furthermore, a DLT solution focuses on scalability, security while lending credence to data transparency in a privacy induced manner. A DLT solution has shortcomings as mentioned in the previous section, however, these shortcomings are overshadowed by the potential benefits that DLT technology would bring to lead times and efficiency of large-scale, pension administration.

When looking to the cross assessment of the STS model and Structuration theory, we need to consider what will truly bring about a system that is not only on paper malleable but adaptable in a real-world environment to the shaping and reshaping of systemic pension structures (of which the assumed solution would be a part of). DLT meets the basis of these requirements better as a decentralised solution that is more democratic than an instituted system that limits access points due to centralisation risk.

Overall, the benefits of DLT are much greater when compared to cloud-based technology on a one-to-one basis and results in DLT being selected as a better option for a longer-term solution.

6.6 DLT Solution Layers and Applicability to a DLT Based Pension Solution

In identifying a DLT based pension solution as more efficient, we need to further look to a systemic breakdown of how such a solution works in the decentralised finance space as the basis of idea provides a clear parallel to pension provision. This is done by taking a standard approach to DLT solutions in the creation of a layer approach based on levels such as the following proposal from Schär (2021) "Decentralized Finance: On Blockchain and Smart Contract-Based Financial Markets" (Fig. 6.1):

In specifically looking at the bottom 4 layers (Layer 1, 3, and 4) which form the foundational tech stack, in a pension scenario one is able to propose the following 3 layers specifically for the Pension administration space that would in a manner function similar to that which is proposed by Schär and widely accepted. This would function similar to the generalised definitions above; however it would create a framework that will become the foundational basis for pension administration, security, transparency and accessibility by many in usage of the systems (Fig. 6.2).

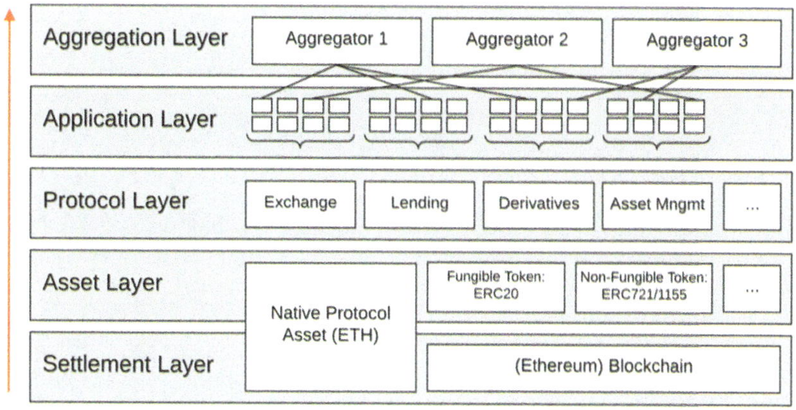

Fig. 6.1 The DeFI Stack in Blockchain

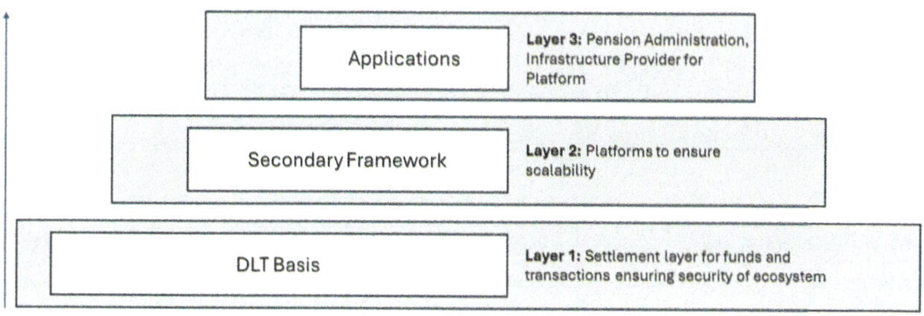

Fig. 6.2 Layered Approach to a future pension solution

In drawing a parallel to Schär's proposal, the Layer 1 (Settlement Layer) would become the settlement layer for the funds and transactions in the pension system. Layer 2 listed above is akin to the Protocol Layer (Layer 3 in Schär's example), which in a decentralised finance scenario gives the ability for specific actions to take place (e.g. Smart Contracts). In a DLT pension solution, this would be the ability for smart contracts that would manage transfers or run actions based on prompts specific to the pension holder's requests or needs for transactions. In the final parallel, one would take the layer 4 of the Schär proposal and equate this to creating a form of user interface/infrastructure for the pension platform.

7 Solution

The proposition based on research, expert interviews, an analysis of the current system and cross comparison identifies DLT as the ideal solution for the creation of a more efficient, large scale pension administration within the second pillar of pensions. More specifically, DLT lends itself perfectly to systematically providing a solution for DC based contribution plans for tracking and usage.

The additional basis for the solution is to look back to our initially introduced theoretical frameworks: the STS theory and Structuration theory. We need to ensure that we consider the interactions of structure, task, technology and people while also focusing on open system approaches and joint optimisation. This, naturally, in addition to the direct socioeconomic engagements of the individuals which interact with the wider pension structure. The best path to interaction and most open path will lead to a successful solution that can be initially rolled out, but also flexible to meet the demands of different stakeholders.

The implementation of such a solution would aim to simplify the end-to-end time transaction while working within the current system of pension provision (looking to reduce the overall lead time that was identified in *Fig. 4.1* while also considering the various stakeholders in the process as mentioned in the structure section*)*. In considering all of these elements, our proposed solution would leverage a decentralised framework to create 3 significant pillars: a GUI, Blockchain Platform and Blockchain Transfer Agency (Fig. 7.1, Fig. 7.2).

When we look to the Graphical User Interface (GUI), it serves its function from the user perspective. Since there is a clear interaction between individuals on the pension holder end and the pension structure it is necessary to provide a solution that also takes care of their interactions with the pension system. Specifically, we identified problems in the pension holders moving across companies

B. Terzic and N. King, *A DLT Solution for Efficient Large-Scale Pension Administration*, BestMasters, https://doi.org/10.1007/978-3-658-48591-7_7

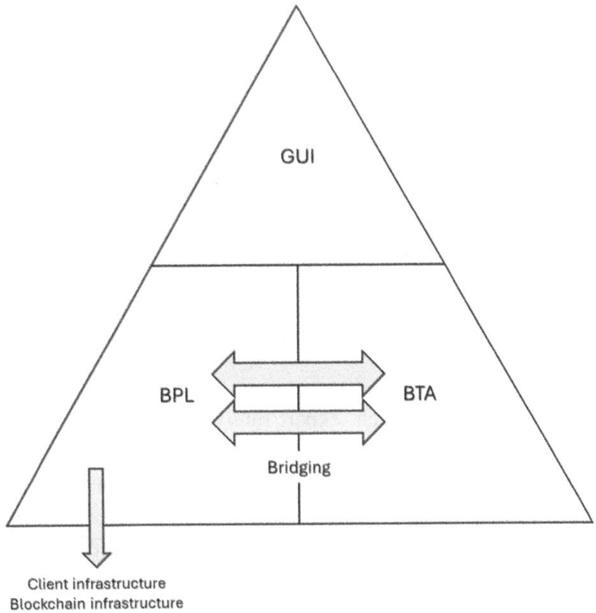

Fig. 7.1 Importance of the triumvirate in pension solutions

Fig. 7.2 Depth of solution discovery

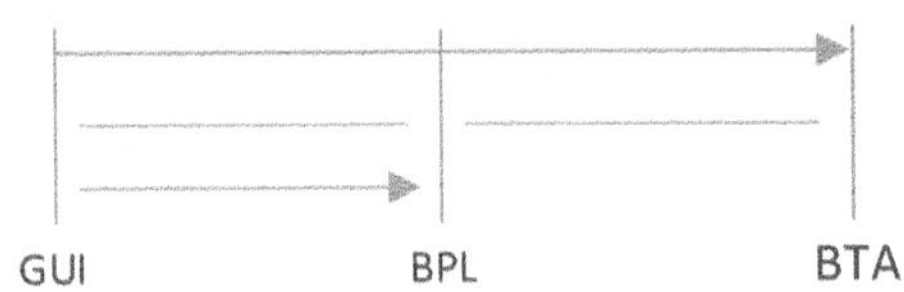

with limited transparency and access to their pension pot holdings. This would be an outward facing, login capable solution in which a pension holder is able to access at any given time their information (even to run updates which can then be leveraged by the BPL to run address updates, life updates, etc.). Some examples of entries could include a Web 2.0 or Web 3.0 solution as an initial idea for how to allow use to a system which is securing personal information externally. The core idea for the GUI is to allow interaction with the pension system even though the user may no longer actively be contributing to it (e.g. retiree) or a part of a company which is logging the data. In other words, we want to create a system that is an open system (per STS theory) allowing for joint optimisation by the individuals that engage with it. This will also help further the system more forward into the future as the engagement can be direct rather than through a proxy (as we saw with the case study in the individual attempting to transfer a pension which took place over many weeks).

In the same direction, we also indicated the need for a secondary section of the 'triumvirate': The BPL, or Blockchain Platform. This would be the source of the technology that powers the system in the backend. It would be the connection point for corporates, auditors and several other stakeholders listed out in the above section which would require the necessary data transparency to ensure smooth processing of pension provision. Coupled with the GUI, this is especially significant because this is the DLT basis of the system design. It would create an essential technology that ties together all additional aspect of the proposed solution and creates the necessary transparency, data aggregation and singular ledger as mentioned in the cross comparisons with cloud-based technology. The BPL would create a basis for the wider structure and directly ties the task to the stakeholder as we look to the final portion of the pyramid. We believe that our proposed solution as it runs on a basis of distributed ledger technology would bring the necessary changes to create an efficient large-scale pension administration. In addition, the core of the technology, decentralisation is not one that can be overlooked. In assessing the cross-comparisons we did identify this as a positive; more so, when we now look to our proposed solution it makes it even more appealing as the proposed 'triumvirate' is scalable and the nodes for such a system can be widespread with server locations that could be relevant to a scale of pension plan expectations. For example, we identify the need for a minimum number of nodes (15) and a scalable system with more systemic engagement that this amount is scaled up as needed. This will create a functional basis that the system can thrive on.

The final portion of the pyramid is a proposition for a transfer agency (Blockchain Transfer Agency) as a final underlying layer within DLT. This would allow single shared ledgers to be leveraged and transparent fund transfer. In the example identified in Sect. 5.1 (Cash Pension Transfer) and Sect. 5.2 (Fund Unit Pension Transfer), the solution would greatly simplify the approach and connection points that are necessary if it were run on a single, decentralised ledger. This is shown through the calculations below in the working example of a single ledger, in which transactions become significantly reduced and are no longer running across several ledgers.

7.1 Example of a Shared Ledger Across All Transfer Agents and Pension Plans

The examples in Chap. 5 show the inefficiencies created because each of Transfer Agents and Pension Plans involved in the system are operating separate ledgers to represent the holdings of pension plan members.

Rather than maintaining these separate ledgers, it would be more efficient to implement a shared ledger across the various transfer agents operating on behalf of the pooled funds and the pension administrators operating on behalf of the members. This ledger could then track the holdings of each of the members in each fund.

This would improve efficiency in the operational model by reducing the level of manual administration and communication required between pension plans. It would also enable accurate, up-to-date and consistent information to be held about plan members.

The shared ledger would facilitate better pension reporting, particularly where an individual has pensions with more than one pension plan. If each plan is using the same underlying ledger, then it would be straightforward to provide reporting to show the total value of pension assets and also how the assets are invested at an aggregate level, across pension plans and fund. Not only would this help members to better understand the total value of their pension savings, but this transparency will also ensure that investment policy and asset allocation is appropriate at an aggregate level rather than considering each pension separately. Ensuring optimal asset allocation and risk management can result in a better level of pension assets accumulated at retirement. This reporting would also be easily accessible to other stakeholders such as regulators and tax authorities.

The table below gives a stylistic example of how a shared ledger across all Transfer Agents and Pension Plans could be used to store holdings for individual members. Given the number of parties involved, this quickly becomes quite complex.

Transfer Agent	Fund	Pension Plan	Beneficiary	Value
TA 1	Fund 1	PP 1	Our example member	€10,245
			Another member	€xxx
			...	...
		...		
		PP n	Another member	€xxx
			...	...
	Fund 2	PP 1	Another member	€xxx
			...	...
		...		
		PP 3	Our example member	€9,745
			Another member	€xxx
			...	
		...		
		PP n	Another member	€xxx
			...	
	Fund 3	PP 1	Our example member	€21,741
			Another member	€xxx
			...	
		...		

		PP 3	Our example member	€3,333
			Another member	€xxx
			…	
		…		
		PP n	Another member	€xxx
			…	
	…			
TA 2	Fund 33	PP 1	Another member	€xxx
			…	
		…		
		PP 4	Our example member	€5,741
			Another member	€xxx
			…	
		…		
		PP n	Our example member	€7,154
			Another member	€xxx
			…	
	Fund 38	PP 1	Another member	€xxx
			…	
		…		

		PP 4	Our example member	€6,951
			Another member	€xxx
			…	
		…		
		PP n	Another member	€xxx
			…	
	Fund 46	PP 1	Another member	€xxx
			…	
		…		
		PP n	Our example member	€1,743
	Fund 50	PP 1	Another member	€xxx
			…	
		…		
		PP n	Our example member	€5,473
			Another member	€xxx
			…	
…				
	Fund 105	PP 1	Another member	€xxx

			...	
		...		
		PP 3	Our example member	€8,123
			Another member	€xxx
			...	
		...		
		PP n	Another member	€xxx
			...	
TA n	Fund 123	PP 1	Another member	€xxx
			...	
		...		
		PP 4	Our example member	€3,357
			Another member	€xxx
			...	
		...		
		PP n	Another member	€xxx
			...	
	...			

In addition to providing enhanced reporting and transparency, this structure could also allow for much more efficient pension transfers. Under this shared system, all Transfer Agents and Pension Plans are inherently connected and by storing information in one structure, transfers between pension plans simply require an update to the single source of truth.

Not only would this reduce the time required for pension transfers and improve the experience for members, but it could also address some of the funding issues raised by in the interview with the Director of Strategic Initiatives at leading occupational pensions administrator. This could provide significant cost savings in the system which will ultimately benefit members.

Taking our transfer example from the Chap. 5, the updates to facilitate a transfer from PP 3 into PP 1 are as follows:

Transfer Agent	Fund	Pension Plan	Beneficiary	Amount
TA 1	Fund 2	PP 3	Our example member	(€9,745)
TA 1	Fund 2	PP 1	Our example member	€9,745
TA 1	Fund 3	PP 3	Our example member	(€3,333)
TA 1	Fund 3	PP 1	Our example member	€3,333
TA n	Fund 105	PP 3	Our example member	(€8,123)
TA n	Fund 105	PP 1	Our example member	€8,123

After these updates, the shared ledger is as follows:

Transfer Agent	Fund	Pension Plan	Beneficiary	Value
TA 1	Fund 1	PP 1	Our example member	€10,245
			Another member	€xxx
			…	…
		…		
		PP n	Another member	€xxx
			…	…
	Fund 2	PP 1	Our example member	€9,745
			Another member	€xxx
			…	…
		…		
		PP n	Another member	€xxx
			…	
	Fund 3	PP 1	Our example member	€25,074
			Another member	€xxx
			…	
		…		
		PP n	Another member	€xxx
			…	

	…			
TA 2	Fund 33	PP 1	Another member	€xxx
			…	
		…		
		PP 4	Our example member	€5,741
			Another member	€xxx
			…	
		…		
		PP n	Our example member	€7,154
			Another member	€xxx
			…	
	Fund 38	PP 1	Another member	€xxx
			…	
		…		
		PP 4	Our example member	€6,951
			Another member	€xxx
			…	
		…		
		PP n	Another member	€xxx
			…	

	Fund 46	PP 1	Another member	€xxx
			…	
		…		
		PP n	Our example member	€1,743
	Fund 50	PP 1	Another member	€xxx
			…	
		…		
		PP n	Our example member	€5,473
			Another member	€xxx
			…	
…				
TA n	Fund 105	PP 1	Our example member	€8,123
			Another member	€xxx
			…	
		…		
		PP n	Another member	€xxx
			…	
	Fund 123	PP 1	Another member	€xxx

			...	
		...		
		PP 4	Our example member	€3,357
			Another member	€xxx
			...	
		...		
		PP n	Another member	€xxx
			...	
	...			

This transfer on a shared ledger would be able to complete almost immediately as it would not require all of the manual communication and coordination required by the current system based on many separate ledgers.

7.2 Solution Implementation & Criticisms

The proposed solution would bring the necessary change to the landscape in the current pension environment, if implemented. The critical point which we must discuss is the rollout of any solution within the pension space, but also within this concept the rollout of a DLT based pension solution specifically. In general, whenever there is existing infrastructure and technology the road to implementation and rollout is met with operational concerns. We even noted this in our expert interviews as all three mentioned the existence of legacy infrastructure which would limit the speed of deployment due to legacy hurdles of data migration, informational archiving, and processes. This is coupled with the mentions of general hesitance towards new, 'untested' technologies in a space that is considered to be relatively slow moving and stable as an industry. The alternative of cloud technology could be seen in a more positive light rather than DLT technology as the adoption rates of cloud topics is much higher than the current state of DLT, which remains exploratory. On the other hand, it can also be viewed as a race to first implementation and whichever entity is able to run the first DLT implementation is able to be more competitive than other entities. Additionally, we could see hesitance in implementation due to the general low risk tolerance in the pension industry and a highly regulated environment. To some extent, this is already visible in other industries where DLT and/or blockchain technology receives secondary status to other solutions simply due to the low implementation rates. Also, due to the regulatory hurdles, the first to implement may be exposed to additional audit scrutiny or assumptions in the regulatory space due to codified law not being written for DLT use. For example, regulation is either repurposed from written law or new law is written to catch up to the field; the first DLT implementation may benefit from a first-mover advantage, however the law may catch up limiting the extent of its use or straining the resources of the system that implementation costs outweigh any foreseeable benefits. Overall, while we still believe that the solution we propose is the best solution, we need to ensure that implementation challenges are considered as they will drive the practical use cases for a DLT solution in efficient pension administration.

Conclusion

8

STS theory and Structuration theory form a cradle that when coupled with the specific case studies, research performed, expert interviews create a holistic assessment. This assessment provides an interesting viewpoint in the exploration to understand whether there are (if any) efficiency gains offered by a potential DLT solution for pension administration. Based on a review of existing technologies, we came to understand that DLT offers the best solution that can be implemented to resolve core issues that plague the current pension landscape and aid in reducing the technical debt which was built up over time.

8.1 Limitations of the Study

We believe that this research provides an essential and valuable insight into a DLT based pension solution for efficient and large-scale pension administration, there are limitations that we need to acknowledge in the course of the study. While many were mentioned and captured in the previous sections, we can summarise the limitations to the following main areas:

1. **Limitation in available research**—includes both limitations in field specific research, limited experts in the field and limitation in available data tied to specific figures. E.g. pensioners living abroad had to be sourced individually and not from the same year which created figures being compared from several different points in time.

B. Terzic and N. King, *A DLT Solution for Efficient Large-Scale Pension Administration*, BestMasters, https://doi.org/10.1007/978-3-658-48591-7_8

2. **Limitation in practical DLT, Pension implementations**—there is a lack of field-based examples that we can draw on for comparison. Since the idea we present in the pages of this thesis is more novel, there are only theoretical examples that we need to base our understanding on. There are no field tests (publicly available) of such a solution.
3. **Limitation in technological evolution**—due to the fields of blockchain and DLT being extremely fast-evolving, findings can be outdated quickly. In other words, by the time a reader engages with this research our proposed solution could be obsolete due to the fast-paced environment. This also ties in directly to a limitation in the ability to standardise an approach for the technology as the field can evolve quickly where basic understandings and approaches need to be adjusted within an implementation proposal.
4. **Limitation in resources**—both time and resource constraints due to the length of this study we were restricted in engaging and research further case studies that would be useful for such research. For example, we could have found and identified more countries to review on a country-based level rather than just the Netherlands and the UK case studies.
5. **Regulatory Uncertainty**—due to the nature of DLT and blockchain still classified as emerging technologies, regulations are still trailing behind implementation cases which can result in the environment having a direct impact on any relevance of the findings. Solution we have proposed is based on current regulations given these are emerging technologies and regulations are evolving rapidly. It is possible that such solutions may be regulated in their implementation in the future. A direct example could be data regulations surrounding a distributed ledger or in the pension regulator limiting the use of the technology while it remains untested for the pension field.

While there are limitations that need to be discussed and indicated, it is also important to note that the method of research we undertook was also meant to both identify and resolve as much as possible the limitations that were listed above. The intent is to recognise the limitations and create scenarios in which these can be balanced by additional case studies or research efforts.

8.2 Further Recommendations for Study

While we engaged in extensive assessments there are further studies and recommendations for future study which will bring further depth and development to bridge theory and practice for DLT in the pension ecosystem. One potential suggestion is to take this body of work and expand on the potential use cases that may exist in the other pillars of the pension system or even further work within the second pillar; for example, a look into how such a system could improve the first pillar of state-provided pension or within the pillar shift the focus on DB pension plans. A further recommendation would be to take the current theoretical framework created in this work to run a proof-of-concept to bind the idea to a practical implementation. This could be possible through several iterations of testing and cycle of 'most viable product' development to reach a working model for the DLT solution and ensuring that the design matches what is occurring within the real world. Finally, to build on the theoretical basis of work it would be recommended to identify how such an implementation may occur in further detail. More specifically, how the transition from current systems would be cutover to a new DLT solution; this is akin to the large overhauls of the current system in a handful of areas to run an updated framework on the cloud. By itself this has led to a subfield of study which recognises the best and proposes the most effective ways for such a cutover into a production scenario. Potential areas of interest with this research would be focuses on how the merging of ledgers (or transition to the single ledger), data transparency and malleability transformations and a general transition from the current system.

8.3 Further Recommendations for Pension Process Stakeholders

There are additional recommendations that can be made from the point of view of stakeholders, namely policymakers and pension administrators. On the regulatory end with policymakers, with the introduction of this technology they may need to review how to create policy for administration and usage of a single ledger. Due to the technical debt of the pension industry many of the policies have not caught up to the technical revolutions. More specifically, regulatory concerns on ensuring fair provisioning of pensions will be necessary (which we expect will actually be more straightforward due to a single ledger) and creating audit procedures based on a singular solution. On the pension administrators end, such solutions would not only be competitive on the market; they would also bolster offerings and efficiency gains from the administrator's perspective. Specifically due to the single ledger, we may find that this increases efficiency gains to such a great extent that administrators need to review basic pension plan setups that were created around burdensome processes. For further studies by the Pension administrators, we would recommend running a parallel run process where they run the processes as is today and they run a parallel process in a DLT sandbox to identify specific efficiency gains of the process one-to-one. This would provide the space with clear, comparable values and further enhance the ability for pension administrators to oversee pension provision.

We recognise that many of the stakeholders are operating in a highly regulated environment and are also large organisations that can be highly risk-averse, slow-moving and resistant to change. We therefore propose that the 'end state' solution that we have described given could be implemented in two steps. The first step to implement a platform for the sharing of information on a 'read-only' basis (akin to the UK Pensions Dashboard Programme). This would allow some efficiency gains and allow stakeholders to interact in a very risk-controlled way.

Once all stakeholders are comfortable with the read-only shared infrastructure and this has demonstrated the expected value, they should progress to the full 'read/write' shared ledger. This approach is also likely to be preferable to regulators as they are able to monitor progress and evolve regulations over time as the solutions become proven. We recommend that based on this, regulators create a sandbox in which pension administrators are encouraged to test a DLT solution. A solution like this is in the best interest of all stakeholders in the process and could provide much needed relief to the pension field.

8.4 Implications of the DLT Pension Solution

There is a great deal of potential as has been provided for a future of DLT based pension solutions in increasing the efficiency of administration for pension systems. Through the case studies that we specifically assessed in the United Kingdom and Netherlands; such systems would directly benefit through DLT based administration. As both hinge on swathes of data and transparency, the stakeholders in the systems would benefit both in offering such a solution and from a user's perspective. DLT is proven to be able to handle large data sets on a single ledger, especially so in recent years with the changes to pension administration from a policy and increased complexity perspective. If no new technologies are introduced to be able to coincide with minor pension revolutions than the technical debt will be further and further built up until a collapse of an important structural system ensues through all 3 pillars.

Through technological revolution, we need to ensure that the future of pension systems is organised and that not only technically but humanitarianly the systems continue to provide essential survival for persons into their senior years. In order to ensure freedoms that humans need to be entitled too, we need to ensure the longstanding support of a robust pension system with the necessary technical prowess. Otherwise, we are subject to failures. If we remind ourselves of Lewitt's Diamond model, one failure in a system causes a completely dependent failure of the other areas. Let us at least attempt to control the one area for a better future, technology.

References

Adamczyk, A. (2024, July 7). *Fortune*. Retrieved from Boomers are leaving America to retire abroad in droves because the U.S. is just too expensive: https://fortune.com/2024/07/07/americans-retire-abroad-cheap-healthcare-spain-europe/

AiCIO. (2017, Oct). *Dutch pensions adapt blockchain tech for fund administration*. Retrieved from ProQuest: https://www.proquest.com/trade-journals/dutch-pensions-adapt-blockchain-tech-fund/docview/2194208777/se-2

Al-Thobhani, N. (2017). *Implementation of cloud computing in the General Authority for Insurance and Pensions.*

Archer, M. S. (1995). *Realist Social Theory: The Morphogenetic Approach.* Cambridge: Cambridge University Press.

Benna, T. (2003). The Problem Isn't the 401(k)--the Problem is How to Invest It. *Journal of Financial Planning, 16*(1).

Blommestein, H. J. (2009). Moving Beyond the 'DB Vs. DC' Debate: The Appeal of Hybrid Pension Plans. *Rotman International Journal of Pension Management, 2*(2).

Breit, E., & Salomon, R. (2015). Making the Technological Transition – Citizens' Encounters with Digital Pension Services. *Social Policy & Administration*, 299–315.

Centraal Buereau voor de Statistiek. (2007, February 20). *Centraal Buereau voor de Statistiek*. Retrieved from One in eleven old age pensioners live abroad: https://www.cbs.nl/en-gb/news/2007/08/one-in-eleven-old-age-pensioners-live-abroad

citigroup. (2023). *Pension Reform in The Netherlands—'Wet Toekomst Pensionen'*. Retrieved from https://www.citigroup.com/rcs/citigpa/storage/public/icpublic/Pension%20Reform%20in%20the%20Netherlands.pdf

Currency Fair. (2023, January 24). *Currency Fair*. Retrieved from Why are so many Americans choosing to retire abroad?: https://blog.currencyfair.com/consumer/why-are-so-many-americans-choosing-to-retire-abroad

Deutsche Rentenversicherung. (2024). *Deutsche Rentenversicherung*. Retrieved from International: https://www.deutsche-rentenversicherung.de/DRV/EN/International/international_node.html

Downes, S. (2024, April 30). *FT Adviser*. Retrieved from Financial Times: https://www.ftadviser.com/pensions/2024/04/30/shocking-tech-leaves-pensions-industry-in-precarious-position/

B. Terzic and N. King, *A DLT Solution for Efficient Large-Scale Pension Administration*, BestMasters, https://doi.org/10.1007/978-3-658-48591-7

Emery, R. (2024, September 11). *MoneyWeek*. Retrieved from Retiring abroad: What to consider, from tax to pensions: https://moneyweek.com/personal-finance/retiring-abroad-finances

Giddens, A. (1984). *The constitution of society: Outline of the theory of structuration.* . Cambridge: Polity Press.

Immigration Department of Malaysia—Ministry of Home Affairs. (2024). *Immigratoin Department of Malaysia*. Retrieved from Malaysia My Second Home (MM2H): https://www.imi.gov.my/index.php/en/main-services/malaysia-my-second-home-mmh2-en/

International Labour Organization. (2024). *Pensions*. Retrieved from ILO.org: https://www.ilo.org/universal-social-protection-department/areas-work-social-protection-department/policy-development-and-applied-research/pensions

Kamal, M., Abdullah, C. M., Shaiara, F., Kamal, A. R., Hasan, M. M., Kim, J.-S., & Hossain, M. A. (2023). Blockchain-Based Pension System Ensuring Security, Provenance and Efficiency. *IEICE Transactions on Information and Systems*, 1085–1088.

Kranz, J. J., Hanelt, A., & Kolbe, L. M. (2016). Understanding the influence of absorptive capacity and ambidexterity on the process of business model change – the case of on-premise and cloud-computing software. *Information Systems Journal*, 477–517.

Kuhn, R., Yaga, D., & Voas, J. (2019). Rethinking Distributed Ledger Technology. *IEEE Computer*, 68–72.

Logan, O. (2023, June 22). *I Am Expat*. Retrieved from An increasing number of German pension recipients are retiring abroad: https://www.iamexpat.de/career/employment-news/an-increasing-number-german-pension-recipients-are-retiring-abroad#:~:text=Of%20the%2020%20million%20pensioners,higher%20than%2020%20years%20ago.

Mierzejewski, A. C. (2016). *A History of the German Public Pension System: Continuity amid Change*. Rowman & Littlefield.

OECD. (2024). *Recommendation of the Council forthe Good Design of Defined Contribution Pension Plans*. Retrieved from OECD.org: https://legalinstruments.oecd.org/api/print?ids=673&lang=en

Pasmore et al. (1982). Sociotechnical Systems: A North American Reflection on Empirical Studies of the Seventies. *Human Relations*, 1179–1204. Retrieved from Sage Journals: https://journals.sagepub.com/doi/10.1177/001872678203501207

Pensions Policy Institute. (2022, Oct). *Lost Pensions 2022: What's the scale and impact?* Retrieved from pensionspolicyinstitute.org.uk: https://www.pensionspolicyinstitute.org.uk/media/yxgdozgx/202210-bn134-lost-pensions-2022-whats-the-scale-and-impact.pdf

Regeringskansliet. (2020). *The Swedish pension system and pension projections until 2070*. Retrieved from https://economy-finance.ec.europa.eu/system/files/2021-05/se_-_ar_2021_final_pension_fiche.pdf

Rijksoverheid Nederland. (2023, July 01). Wet toekomst pensioenen in werking. Retrieved from https://www.rijksoverheid.nl/actueel/nieuws/2023/07/01/wet-toekomst-pensioenen-in-werking

Sarker, I., & Datta, B. (2022). Re-designing the pension business processes for achieving technology-driven reforms through blockchain adoption: A proposed architecture. *Technological Forecasting and Social Change*.

Savas et al. (2023). Migrating to a new country in late life: A review of the literature on international retirement migration. *Demographic Research, 48*, 233–270. Retrieved from https://www.demographic-research.org/volumes/vol48/9/48-9.pdf

Schär, F. (2021). Decentralized Finance: On Blockchain- and Smart Contract-Based Financial Markets. *Federal Reserve Bank of St. Louis REVIEW*, 153–174.

Schubert, S.-C., & Perret, J. K. (2024, Feb 20). *Opportunities and Limitations of Private Pension Plans based on Blockchain Technologies (Chancen und Grenzen der privaten Altersvorsorge auf Basis von Blockchain-Technologien).* Retrieved from SSRN: https://papers.ssrn.com/sol3/papers.cfm?abstract_id=4733102

Sestoft, P. (2017, Mar 27). *Autonomous pension funds on the blockchain.* Retrieved from IT University of Copenhagen: https://itu.dk/~sestoft/papers/autonomous-pensions.pdf

Shabani, A. (2023, December 21). *Schengen News.* Retrieved from Brits Are Increasingly Choosing to Retire Abroad as More Than 200k Seniors Chose to Live in EU: https://schengen.news/brits-are-increasingly-choosing-to-retire-abroad-as-more-than-200k-seniors-chose-to-live-in-eu/

Stanke, J., Unterberg, M., Trauth, D., & Bergs, T. (2020). Development of a hybrid DLT cloud architecture for the automated use of finite element simulation as a service for fine blanking. *The International Journal of Advanced Manufacturing Technology*, 3717–3724.

Taylor, J. (2024, May 9). *The Guardian.* Retrieved from Google Cloud accidentally deletes UniSuper's online account due to 'unprecedented misconfiguration': https://www.theguardian.com/australia-news/article/2024/may/09/unisuper-google-cloud-issue-account-access

Terziev, V. (2019). Historical Development and Characteristics of Pension Systems. *IJASOS—International E-Journal of Advances in Social Sciences*, 124–135.

The United States Social Security Administration. (2024). *U.S. International Social Security Agreements.* Retrieved from https://www.ssa.gov/international/agreements_overview.html?tl=0

Trautmann, K. (2023, May 5). *The Evolution of Cloud Computing and Distributed Ledger Technology.* Retrieved from ISACA: https://www.isaca.org/resources/news-and-trends/isaca-now-blog/2023/the-evolution-of-cloud-computing-and-distributed-ledger-technology

UK Government. (2021, Sep 21). *Workplace pension participation and savings trends of eligible employees: 2009 to 2020.* Retrieved from GOV.UK: https://www.gov.uk/government/statistics/workplace-pension-participation-and-savings-trends-2009-to-2020/workplace-pension-participation-and-savings-trends-of-eligible-employees-2009-to-2020

UK Government. (2022, Oct 27). *Summary: Workplace pensions and Automatic Enrolment: employers' perspectives 2022.* Retrieved from GOV.uk: https://www.gov.uk/government/publications/workplace-pensions-and-automatic-enrolment-employers-perspectives-2022/summary-workplace-pensions-and-automatic-enrolment-employers-perspectives-2022

UK Government. (2023a, Jul 11). *Addressing the challenge of deferred small pots: a call for evidence.* Retrieved from GOV.UK: https://www.gov.uk/government/consultations/addressing-the-challenge-of-deferred-small-pots/addressing-the-challenge-of-deferred-small-pots-a-call-for-evidence#:~:text=call%2Dfor%2Devidence-,Introduction,(%20AE%20)%20workplace%20pensions%20market.

UK Government. (2023b, Nov 22). *Ending the proliferation of deferred small pots.* Retrieved from GOV.UK: https://www.gov.uk/government/consultations/ending-the-proliferation-of-deferred-small-pension-pots/ending-the-proliferation-of-deferred-small-pots

UK Government. (2023c, Nov 22). *Government response to ending the proliferation of deferred small pots.* Retrieved from GOV.UK: https://www.gov.uk/government/consultations/ending-the-proliferation-of-deferred-small-pension-pots/outcome/government-response-to-ending-the-proliferation-of-deferred-small-pots
UK Government. (2023d, Nov 22). *Looking to the future: greater member security and rebalancing risk.* Retrieved from GOV.UK: https://www.gov.uk/government/calls-for-evidence/looking-to-the-future-greater-member-security-and-rebalancing-risk/looking-to-the-future-greater-member-security-and-rebalancing-risk
United Nations—Population Division. (2020). *United Nations.* Retrieved from International Migrant Stock: https://www.un.org/development/desa/pd/content/international-migrant-stock
Verbon, H. (1987). *The Rise and Evolution of Public Pension Systems.* Amsterdam: Springer Nature.
Verbon, H. (2012). *The Evolution of Public Pension Schemes.* Springer Berlin Heidelberg.
Westerlund, M., & Kratzke, N. (2018). Towards Distributed Clouds: A Review About the Evolution of Centralized Cloud Computing, Distributed Ledger Technologies, and A Foresight on Unifying Opportunities and Security Implications. *2018 International Conference on High Performance Computing & Simulation (HPCS).*
Wigand, D. (2007). Building on Leavitt's Diamond Model of Organizations: The Organizational Interaction Diamond Model and the Impact of Information Technology on Structure, People, and Tasks. *Americas Conference on Information Systems (AMCIS).*
World Bank Group. (2023). Population ages 65 and above (% of total population). Retrieved from https://data.worldbank.org/indicator/SP.POP.65UP.TO.ZS?end=2023&start=1960
World Economic Forum. (2019, Jun). *Investing in (and for) Our Future.* Retrieved from https://www3.weforum.org/docs/WEF_Investing_in_our_Future_report_2019.pdf

The manufacturer's authorised representative in the EU is Springer Nature Customer Service Centre GmbH, Europaplatz 3, 69115 Heidelberg, Germany. If you have any concerns regarding our products, please contact ProductSafety@springernature.com

Printed and bound by CPI Group (UK) Ltd, Croydon, CR0 4YY
30/09/2026
02225263-0001